AMAZING GRACE

Publications International, Ltd.

Scripture quotations from *The Holy Bible, King James Version*

Images from Shutterstock.com

Louis Weber, CEO
Publications International, Ltd.
8140 Lehigh Avenue
Morton Grove, IL 60053

ISBN: 978-1-63938-865-3

Manufactured in China.

8 7 6 5 4 3 2 1

CONTENTS

GETTING AND GIVING GRACE

Prayer acts as a conversation with God—where we share our hopes, dreams, fears, and heartaches with the only one who fully understands us. God wants to be a part of our lives. He wants us to turn to him whenever we feel weak, scared, or alone, and need someone who can help us.

There is no right way to pray. Some of the loveliest prayers are the most simple in language. Prayers can be whispered, put into song, shouted out to the heavens, or simply said in one's heart. There is no wrong time to talk to God.

We pray whenever we create space in our day to share with God. We pray with our words, but we can also pray through our actions. God not only knows our minds, but he sees the depths of our hearts, our true selves. In seeing what we really are, he always knows what we need.

Let this book remind you to pause for a moment and know that God is near. In moments of praise and gratitude or in moments of hardship and despair, God's Word holds true: "I am with you always." The blessings and grace we receive every day serve as reminders of this divine promise.

JANUARY

JANUARY 1

But the God of all grace, who hath called us unto his eternal glory by Christ Jesus, after that ye have suffered a while, make you perfect, stablish, strengthen, settle you.

—1 Peter 5:10

God's grace is not just for the good times. It is also sufficient for our suffering, giving us new insights and strengths. O God of all grace, give us grace for each moment of need and abundance so we can see your glory and plan more clearly.

JANUARY 2

For the grace of God that bringeth salvation hath appeared to all men.

—Titus 2:11

God's grace is for everyone, or at least for everyone looking. Look for it and receive it. Once you see grace, you will see it in the sky above, and you will see it in the plants around you. You will hear it in the words you hear and the faces that you see. It is everywhere evident and always free. It's grace, after all.

JANUARY 3

For I know the thoughts that I think toward you, saith the Lord, thoughts of peace, and not of evil, to give you an expected end.

—Jeremiah 29:11

JANUARY 4

He that loveth pureness of heart, for the grace of his lips the king shall be his friend.

—Proverbs 22:11

Lord, give me a pure heart and a kind tongue. Then the king of glory will be my friend, helper, and guide. And then my reputation will reflect my integrity, and my influence will reflect your glory.

JANUARY 5

It is of the Lord's mercies that we are not consumed, because his compassions fail not.

They are new every morning: great is thy faithfulness.

The Lord is my portion, saith my soul; therefore will I hope in him.

—Lamentations 3:22–24

JANUARY 6

A new heart also will I give you, and a new spirit will I put within you: and I will take away the stony heart out of your flesh, and I will give you an heart of flesh.

—Ezekiel 36:26

JANUARY 7

I thank my God always on your behalf, for the grace of God which is given you by Jesus Christ.

—1 Corinthians 1:4

Do this today. Text or email someone and tell them you thank God for them. In what specific ways has God shown grace to you through their care, kindness, or compassion? He gave them the motivation and the resources they have extended to you. Say thanks.

JANUARY 8

Walk in the light! So you shall know
that fellowship of love.
His Spirit only can bestow,
who reigns in light above.
Walk in the light! And you shall find
your heart made truly his,
who dwells in cloudless light enshrined,
in whom no darkness is.
Walk in the light! And yours shall be
a path, though thorny, bright.
For God, by grace, shall dwell in thee,
and God himself is light.

—Bernard Barton, Adapted

JANUARY 9

But Noah found grace in the eyes of the Lord.

—Genesis 6:8

Mercy is not something we need beg of you, O God, for your pleasure is to love us. Mercy, grace, and love are always available to us, Lord, for you are always available to us.

JANUARY 10

But by the grace of God I am what I am: and his grace which was bestowed upon me was not in vain; but I laboured more abundantly than they all: yet not I, but the grace of God which was with me.

—1 Corinthians 15:10

The grace of the living God refreshes like cool, clear water on a hot day, giving our parched souls the sustenance and nourishment they need.

JANUARY 11

Move our hearts with the calm, smooth flow of your grace. Let the river of your love run through our souls. May my soul be carried by the current of your love, towards the wide, infinite ocean of heaven. Stretch out my heart with your strength, as you stretch out the sky above the earth. Smooth out any wrinkles of hatred or resentment. Enlarge my soul that it may know more fully your truth.

—Gilbert of Hoyland

JANUARY 12

God hears my cries for help, and
He answers every prayer.
I only need be patient—
He supplies the "how" and "where."
Sometimes it may be immediate
In a tangible way I'll know;
While other times I wait assured
That he is strengthening my soul.
His grace is all-sufficient
To meet my heart-cries need.
As I lean upon his promises,
Walking in faith, he'll lead.

JANUARY 13

And thou shalt speak unto all that are wise hearted, whom I have filled with the spirit of wisdom, that they may make Aaron's garments to consecrate him, that he may minister unto me in the priest's office.

—Exodus 28:3

Growing in wisdom means growing in love, tolerance, grace, and acceptance.

JANUARY 14

Today, may I feel grateful for those moments when something heavenly graces my daily routine.

JANUARY 15

Now therefore, I pray thee, if I have found grace in thy sight, shew me now thy way, that I may know thee, that I may find grace in thy sight: and consider that this nation is thy people.

—Exodus 33:13

When it seems like God is treating you like a favorite child, that's grace.

JANUARY 16

Ere we reach the shining river,
Lay we every burden down;
Grace our spirits will deliver,
And provide a robe and crown.
Yes, we'll gather at the river,
The beautiful, the beautiful river —
Gather with the saints at the river
That flows by the throne of God.
Soon we'll reach the shining river,
Soon our pilgrimage will cease,
Soon our happy hearts will quiver
With the melody of peace.
Yes, we'll gather at the river,
The beautiful, the beautiful river —
Gather with the saints at the river
That flows by the throne of God.

—Robert Lowry

JANUARY 17

Who hath saved us, and called us with an holy calling, not according to our works, but according to his own purpose and grace, which was given us in Christ Jesus before the world began.

—2 Timothy 1:9

You have a calling today to be faithful as a parent, employee, or friend. This calling is holy, a way of worshipping, as you see even ordinary responsibilities fulfilling God's purpose. The way you change a diaper or encourage a subordinate may change the world some day. Depend on the amazing grace of God to do this with joy. It was always his plan.

JANUARY 18

Though I cannot see you, angel dear,
I know that you are there.
Though I cannot hear you speak,
I sense you loud and clear.
For in my heart I recognize
the pattern of your call.
And in your wings I've found
a gentle place to fall.
Should I attempt to see you, angel dear,
I know that I will fail.
Should I attempt to pin you down,
I know I won't prevail.
For in my soul I've come to know
your presence is discerned.
And through my faith I understand
your mercy must be earned.
If ever I am lonely, angel dear,
I know you're close at hand.
If ever I am frightened,
I know that by me you will stand.
For in the quiet of the night
I sense your loving grace
and rest in peaceful comfort
in your heavenly embrace.

JANUARY 19

I thought I heard an angel
whisper in my ear,
telling me which way to go
and that she'd guide me there.
I thought I felt a wisp of wing
brush against my arm,
surrounding me with loving grace
to keep me free from harm.
I thought I saw an angel
dancing through the air,
spreading joy to all below
who called to her in prayer.
I thought I met an angel
in a loving, caring friend,
there for me through thick and thin,
loyal until the end.
I thought I touched an angel
in the arms of one I love,
enfolded in the gentle glow
of blessings from above.

JANUARY 20

Wrapped within your shield of wings,
I feel protected from all harm.
Beneath your ever-watchful eyes,
I live in peaceful comfort.
Held against your beating heart,
I know that I am deeply loved.
Carried in your mighty arms,
I become more confident and strong.
Guided by your sage advice,
I find direction for my life.
Prompted by your inspiration,
I let my inner artist dream.
Blessed by your amazing grace,
I wait for miracles fulfilled.
Softened by your gentleness,
I act with kindness and compassion.
Wrapped within your shield of wings,
I know that I am always safe.
Beneath your constant, caring gaze,
I live my life with joy and faith.

JANUARY 21

Heavenly hosts of angels flying,
watching over their precious flocks,
keep each one safe from harm
like gentle, careful shepherds.
Anointed guardians of light,
directing steps of mortal souls,
guide us to our righteous paths
like wise and knowing sages.
Winged wonders of faith and joy,
shining down upon the earth,
fill our hearts with inner warmth
like silver silken moonbeams.
Overlords of hope renewed,
granting gifts of soul's redemption,
shower us with amazing grace
like loyal, caring friends.
Appointed educators,
serving lessons of the heart,
empower us with inspirations
like dedicated teachers.
Heavenly hosts of angels flying,
comforting their precious children,
enfold us in arms so strong
like doting, loving parents.

JANUARY 22

I will mention the lovingkindnesses of the Lord, and the praises of the Lord, according to all that the Lord hath bestowed on us, and the great goodness toward the house of Israel, which he hath bestowed on them according to his mercies, and according to the multitude of his lovingkindnesses.

—Isaiah 63:7

God's loving kindnesses are many. Just mention them today. Some child, friend, or coworker must be reminded of his love. And so must you. Praise the Lord for his goodness and mercy, bestowed freely and generously. It is worth talking about.

JANUARY 23

The love of God gives grace a thousandfold more than human actions deserve. If you give him the merest mite, he will pay you back with gold.

—The Way of a Pilgrim

JANUARY 24

Precious Lord, bless me with your grace that I may experience the deepest peace and healing only you can provide. Show me the merciful love that knows no end that I may rest today knowing I am cared for. Amen.

JANUARY 25

Forgiveness is the central virtue in God's treasure chest—God's forgiveness of us and our forgiveness of others and ourselves. At times we find that forgiveness comes very easily, even for grievous and painful hurts. But many times, we seem powerless to forgive, no matter how hard we try. This is when God's forgiving grace has the opportunity to touch and change us and then be extended to others through our example.

JANUARY 26

Father, it's to you we come,
To pray for loved ones and for friends;
You offer mercy, grace, and peace,
And healing love that never ends.

JANUARY 27

For I am persuaded, that neither death, nor life, nor angels, nor principalities, nor powers, nor things present, nor things to come, Nor height, nor depth, nor any other creature, shall be able to separate us from the love of God, which is in Christ Jesus our Lord.

—Romans 8:38–39

Try to imagine something that can separate you from the love of God. There is nothing else to consider once you eliminate angels, demons, times, places, and others. Death? He's got you. Life? You are still his. Everything in between? That's covered, too. It's going to be alright.

JANUARY 28

And ye shall know the truth,
and the truth shall make you free.

—John 8:32

Peaceful angels rest among us,
Whispering secrets we can hear,
If we'll calm ourselves and listen,
Truth and grace will gather near.

JANUARY 29

Scooting over to make room, God of daily bread, the kids and I greet you over our peanut butter and jelly lunch. Through simple graces and verses to bless childhood fare and bedtime prayers to offer you the day, I'm honored to introduce you to my child.

JANUARY 30

The grace of our Lord Jesus Christ be with your spirit. Amen.

—Philemon 1:25

May the extravagant and outlandish grace of our blessed, powerful, and generous Lord Jesus Christ, who rules and reigns forever and can forgive our sins and change our lives, may the grace of that same Lord Jesus be with your spirit today and always. Amen.

JANUARY 31

Amazing grace! How sweet the sound
that saved a wretch like me!
I once was lost, but now am found;
was blind, but now I see.
The Lord has promised good to me,
his word my hope secures;
he will my shield and portion be,
as long as life endures.

—John Newton, "Amazing Grace"

FEBRUARY

FEBRUARY 1

Thy word is a lamp unto my feet, and a light unto my path.

—Psalm 119:105

FEBRUARY 2

I blew it. Give me courage to admit my mistake, apologize, and go on. Keep me from getting stuck in denial, despair, and, worst of all, fear of trying again. In your remolding hands, God of grace, failures can become feedback and mistakes can simply be lessons in what doesn't work. Remind me that perfection means "suited to the task," not "without mistakes." There's a world of difference.

FEBRUARY 3

In the day when I cried thou answeredst me, and strengthenedst me with strength in my soul.

—Psalm 138:3

FEBRUARY 4

Thou wilt keep him in perfect peace, whose mind is stayed on thee: because he trusteth in thee.

—Isaiah 26:3

FEBRUARY 5

There is in your grace, God of second chances, insufficient evidence to prove my latest setback is a failure. Even if it is, with you, failure is never final but an opportunity to learn and grow. When I goof, as I am prone to do, help me from doubling the problem by failing to take advantage of your redemption.

FEBRUARY 6

Moms know what to do with hamburger, fabric scraps, and winter: Make meatloaf, quilts, and windowsill gardens, showing our children how to live "as if." As if useless can become useful, as if seemingly dead can live, as if spring will come, God's renewing love scattered around like posies in a garden of grace.

FEBRUARY 7

If I am right, Thy grace impart,
Still in the right to stay;
If I am wrong, oh teach my heart
To find that better way.

—Alexander Pope

FEBRUARY 8

Lord, I know that you simply cannot be everywhere at once, so you made angels to help you spread your loving grace upon the earth. Thank you for blessing my life with an abundance of angels in the form of friends and family members who love and care for me. They fill my life with joy and give me wings to follow my dreams.

FEBRUARY 9

A man that hath friends must shew himself friendly: and there is a friend that sticketh closer than a brother.

—Proverbs 18:24

Friendships come about by good fortune, mutual respect, and the grace of God.

FEBRUARY 10

For it is God which worketh in you both to will and to do of his good pleasure.

—Philippians 2:13

FEBRUARY 11

Bless this newborn, Lord, with hunger of soul and mind to match a growing, thriving body. At awesome moments like these, we, your "big children," feel your blessing wrapped around us like a baby's blanket. Give us wisdom, patience, humor, stamina, humility, joy, and grace to pass on.

FEBRUARY 12

Blessed are you who know how to celebrate the goodness of life. Blessed because you choose to see the grace above and beyond the pain. Blessed because you see a potential friend in every stranger you meet. Blessed because you know the darkest clouds have brilliant silver linings. And most blessed because: All you ever knew of the half-empty glass was that it was almost full.

FEBRUARY 13

These are exciting times to be part of your world, O God, for your Spirit is stirring us into vision and action to revitalize our communities. Be with us in difficult times of decision-making. Still the shrill voices of opponents, for we must learn to be united, despite our differences of opinion.

Move us beyond our too-busy schedules, our boredom with routine and committees, our uneasiness in the face of change, and our preference to debate, delegate, and deliberate rather than do. Be with us as we volunteer and vote. Be with and bless us, the ordinary citizens, the salt of the earth, the "every person," for we are as needy as our streets and communities. Needy in spirits that sometimes falter and sigh under the enormity of the task, needy in energy that is so often drained, needy in vision that is sometimes unclear.

Extend your hand of grace and bless us as we revitalize our neighborhoods, communities, and country, keeping you as cornerstone and Master Builder.

FEBRUARY 14

The lord is good, a strong hold in the day of trouble; and he knoweth them that trust in him.

—Nahum 1:7

FEBRUARY 15

And now abideth faith, hope, charity, these three; but the greatest of these is charity.

—1 Corinthians 13:13

What can we say to bless this lonely meal? What words can we use to grace this half-portion of life? Be with me as I swallow around lonely tears. Bless my remembering; inspire me to care for myself in honor of all the love that went before. From now on, I will set places in my heart for Memory and Hope, new companions for my table.

FEBRUARY 16

Father, unity among your people is precious to you—and precious to us as well. We cannot achieve it without your assistance, though. Help us to keep petty disagreements from dividing us. Give us the grace to work through any disagreement with love and understanding.

FEBRUARY 17

Sacrifice doesn't always come easily, Lord. Please show me those opportunities you have placed in my day for me to lay down my own to-do list and be aware of the greater things you are doing through me. Don't let me miss those opportunities, Lord. Please do not allow any grumbling on my part to deter your work. Grant me the grace to make any sacrifices you need from me today.

FEBRUARY 18

Lord, we pray for all those in positions of leadership in our government. The pressures and influences on them are of a magnitude we can only imagine. Watch over them, Lord. Reach out to them with your grace, and instill in them your character, your priorities, and your vision for our country and our world.

FEBRUARY 19

Have not I commanded thee? Be strong and of a good courage; be not afraid, neither be thou dismayed: for the Lord thy God is with thee whithersoever thou goest.

—Joshua 1:9

FEBRUARY 20

Lord, I just want to tell you how much I love you, how grateful I am that you have taken me into your care. Ever since I've entrusted myself to you, you've kept me from becoming entangled in the kinds of things that would bring me to ruin. You fill my heart and mind with peace as I stay close to you. It's a miracle of your grace that I am standing tall today, lifting my praise to you from a heart full of love.

FEBRUARY 21

Lord, today I pray for your grace and mercy to help me to live unselfishly. Putting others first does not come naturally to me, Lord, but with your help, I will stop and think before I speak or act. I'm not at all confident in my ability to do that without you, but I also know that anything is possible when you are involved. Thank you, Lord.

FEBRUARY 22

Forgiveness is a supernatural response to being wronged. Would we know what forgiveness is if God had not shown us by first forgiving us? It seems highly unlikely. That's why real forgiveness—the kind that God extends to us—can only come through God's grace. In our own strength, we may try to forgive someone over and over again, only to call to mind the offense later (for perhaps the hundredth time). But when we ask God to open our hearts, he fills them with his love and makes us capable of full forgiveness.

FEBRUARY 23

But there is forgiveness with thee, that thou mayest be feared.

—Psalm 130:4

Those who don't know you are missing so much, Lord! Life, joy, pleasures are in your hand, and you are eager to give them as gifts to those who come to you. I pray today for those who are lost and searching. Please shine your grace to light their way. Draw them to yourself as only you can.

FEBRUARY 24

Cast me not away from thy presence;
and take not thy holy spirit from me.

—Psalm 51:11

You fulfilled this promise, Lord, when you gave your Holy Spirit to live within those who dedicate their lives to you. Thank you for transforming my heart with your saving grace and for making me sensitive to your Word and your ways. You truly have brought my soul alive—as if from stone to living flesh.

FEBRUARY 25

Sometimes—when I'm lost on this path of life—I sense your presence. It is so comforting to think of you searching tirelessly to find me again. Grant me your grace so I can stay on your paths more steadily. This way, you'll have more time to devote to searching out others!

FEBRUARY 26

Children, obey your parents in the Lord: for this is right.

—Ephesians 6:1

Help me teach my kids how to grow gracefully and excel, Lord of possibilities. Help me pass on to them standards, goals, and a living faith. Steady me as I help them soar; holding them back says I think they can't.

FEBRUARY 27

Father, rainy days can be so difficult with a house full of restless children. Several days of rain in a row can be nearly impossible. It is a challenge to keep everyone occupied with worthwhile activities.

Lord, you send the sun and rain in equal measure. How can I be thankful for one and not the other? Help me see the beauty in both. I ask for your gifts of grace and peace and an extra dose of resourcefulness to help me survive.

FEBRUARY 28

Dear God,

As I rise each day, give me the strength, courage, and patience to do the best I can for my family. All through the day, guide me with your grace and divine direction into right action and right decision. And when the day is done and it is time for me to rest my weary mind and body, take the burden of my troubles from me so that I can sleep. Watch over me and mine throughout the night, and when it is time to arise to a new day, be there for me all over again. Amen.

FEBRUARY 29

Train up a child in the way he should go: and when he is old, he will not depart from it.

—Proverbs 22:6

MARCH

MARCH 1

Help me, God, to see that you gave your love in such a way that even the most wicked person can repent and find new life in your grace and mercy; indeed, that your love calls even the worst sinners to become your children. You created each person with a specific purpose to serve in this world. Help me, Lord, to pray that each person will turn away from evil, turn to you, and become your devoted servant. Amen.

MARCH 2

God, you gave up your own beloved son for me. How could I possibly love with such a sense of sacrifice? Help me be the kind of person who can put the needs of others before my own. Help me give until it hurts. You have sacrificed for me—now let me give of myself in return. I know that in the end, I will be rewarded with your merciful grace. Amen.

MARCH 3

Lord, be my warrior, my guard, my guide. Let your love be the armor that shields me from the slings and arrows of the day. Let your compassion be the blanket that protects me from the cold at night. Lord, be my warrior, my champion, my protector. Let your love surround me like an impenetrable light that nothing can break through to do me harm. Let your grace bring me peace no matter how crazy things are all around me. Lord, be my warrior.

MARCH 4

Lest thou shouldest ponder the path of life, her ways are moveable, that thou canst not know them.

—Proverbs 5:6

Lord,

I seek to understand your will for me, and to follow it with a joyful heart and spirit. Let me feel your presence moving me in the direction you want me to go. Let me be guided in all my ways by your love and kindness. Let me know the power of your grace as you open the right doors for me, and keep me from the things that would bring me sadness and harm. I seek to know your will, Lord, and to live in that will today and always. Amen.

MARCH 5

But that ye may know that the Son of man hath power upon earth to forgive sins, (he said unto the sick of the palsy,) I say unto thee, Arise, and take up thy couch, and go into thine house.

—Luke 5:24

Dear God,

I don't come in prayer to you to ask for total forgiveness, even though I know you do forgive me my sins and mistakes. I ask that in addition to your merciful grace, you also help me to learn from my experience and glean wisdom from my interactions with the people I need to forgive, or need forgiveness from. Without this understanding, I fear I will repeat the same patterns in the future. Forgive me, God, then help me to forgive. But then, please, help me to increase my wisdom and come to a place in life where I don't keep repeating the same mistakes over and over again. Amen.

MARCH 6

When I feel weak, tired, and alone, give me strength, God, to stand up and face the challenges before me with hope, grace, and the power that comes from your presence. Help me, God, to find the courageous lion within.

MARCH 7

Trust in the Lord with all thine heart; and lean not unto thine own understanding. In all thy ways acknowledge him, and he shall direct thy paths.

—Proverbs 3:5–6

Isn't it amazing how just trusting in God's power and grace can heal us? See it, know it, and heal it. What a gift we have been given!

MARCH 8

That being justified by his grace, we should be made heirs according to the hope of eternal life.

—Titus 3:7

MARCH 9

Let me set my compass to your will, Lord. Let me not be afraid to follow you, even if that pits me against the world's values. Give me a humble heart, Lord, so that I will not judge others—but please give me the gift of moral clarity as well, to seek to live by your values and do your will.

MARCH 10

And of his fulness have all we received, and grace for grace. For the law was given by Moses, but grace and truth came by Jesus Christ.

—John 1:16–17

MARCH 11

Jesus, I ask you to please keep drawing me into closer relationship with you. Sometimes I think of my good acts like a running tally: letting someone in ahead of me in traffic gets me a point, donating money to someone in need gets me ten. But that's a small, legalistic way of thinking. Let me do good things not in hope of a reward but simply to pass along the tremendous grace you have granted to me.

MARCH 12

I ask you to cleanse my heart today of all lingering resentments. I say I forgive something, but sometimes I have a hard time letting it go—I want someone to see my side and tell me I was right! Please let me let go of any bitterness or anger I am holding onto, so that I can keep my hands open to receive your mercy and grace.

MARCH 13

And he said, My presence shall go with thee, and I will give thee rest.

—Exodus 33:14

Moses had met with the Lord at the tabernacle, "face to face, as a man speaketh unto his friend" (verse 11). And yet he is still uncertain and anxious. He is not sure how he will lead the people or who will go with him. He says, "shew me now thy way, that I may know thee, that I may find grace in thy sight" (verse 13).

God replies, "My presence shall go with thee." This is enough. It was enough for Moses. It was enough for Joshua when he fought the Lord's battles, enough for David when he sang the Lord's songs. And it is enough for us as we do the Lord's work.

MARCH 14

The young lions do lack, and suffer hunger: but they that seek the Lord shall not want any good thing.

—Psalm 34:10

God's grace does not depend on our strength. The lions may go hungry, but his own lambs do not: "the Lord is my shepherd; I shall not want" (Psalm 23:1). This is a given, rooted in his character. One of his names is Jehovah-Jireh, which means "the Lord will provide."

MARCH 15

For the same Lord over all is rich unto all that call upon him. For whosoever shall call upon the name of the Lord shall be saved.

—Romans 10:12–13

MARCH 16

But God, who is rich in mercy, for his great love wherewith he loved us.

—Ephesians 2:4

We experience these exceeding riches through Christ. Giving does not make him poorer and withholding does not make him richer. There is no limit or barrier to his bounty. It requires only that we call on the name of the Lord.

MARCH 17

The Lord knoweth the days of the upright: and their inheritance shall be for ever. They shall not be ashamed in the evil time: and in the days of famine they shall be satisfied.

—Psalm 37:18–19

Famine was one of the greatest fears of the ancient Hebrews. Crops failed for all kinds of reasons—a lack of rain or swarms of locusts, for example. Famine is described in Ezekiel 5 as one of the four judgments, along with war, disease, and wild animals. Famines were often long, severe, and followed by pestilence. They felt like the end of all grace. Yet God promised to provide for his faithful servants. "I have commanded the ravens to feed thee there," he tells Elijah (1 Kings 17:4). God can provide a table in the wilderness in the shadow of death, as David attests in Psalm 23:4–5. Do not be afraid. In the days of famine you will be satisfied.

MARCH 18

The law of thy mouth is better unto me than thousands of gold and silver.

—Psalm 119:72

God's words are often depicted as treasure: "More to be desired are they than gold, yea, than much fine gold" (Psalm 19:10). They are "pure words: as silver tried in a furnace of earth, purified seven times" (Psalm 12:6). So it is possible to be physically poor but spiritually rich, since the Word of God is as close as our coffee table.

MARCH 19

We have redemption through his blood, the forgiveness of sins, according to the riches of his grace; Wherein he hath abounded toward us in all wisdom and prudence.

—Ephesians 1:7–8

The real and lasting wealth of scripture is more valuable than any other investment. The return is wisdom and insight as well as peace and salvation. This return is better than silver or gold.

MARCH 20

The Lord shall preserve thee from all evil: he shall preserve thy soul. The Lord shall preserve thy going out and thy coming in from this time forth, and even for evermore.

—Psalm 121:7–8

When the unexpected happens, remember this: the Lord will keep you. He will keep you when you are going out and when you are coming in. And he is keeping your very soul. This is certain, even in our uncertainty, and it is very comforting. Because how would it help if a man "shall gain the whole world, and lose his own soul?" Jesus asks this in Mark 8:36. And the answer is, not much. So be glad that he is preserving it. You are being kept by his power and grace. And that is enough.

MARCH 21

Which in other ages was not made known unto the sons of men, as it is now revealed unto his holy apostles and prophets by the Spirit; That the Gentiles should be fellowheirs, and of the same body, and partakers of his promise in Christ by the gospel: Whereof I was made a minister, according to the gift of the grace of God given unto me by the effectual working of his power.

—Ephesians 3:5–7

The good news, which nobody expected, is that everybody is included. We can all partake of the promise in Christ, as the Apostles and prophets declared by the spirit. In Christ, we have a shared inheritance as members of the same body of believers, regardless of background or class or gender. This is an equality unknown in the world before Christ but enjoyed by his people forever. We are one in the Spirit. Amen.

MARCH 22

And Saul said, Blessed be ye of the Lord; for ye have compassion on me.

—1 Samuel 23:21

My kindergarten-age daughter has had a "best friend" since preschool, but recently the other little girl has been unkind to my daughter, pointedly excluding her at recess and talking about her unkindly to the other girls in their class. After more than a month of this behavior, my wife spoke to the other girl's mother, and the woman was defensive, even hostile, intimating that it was our daughter's fault and that she was provoking her child in some way. My wife gently persisted, and as we talked to the other family and our own child, it became apparent that the other little girl is jealous of our daughter's reading ability. Though it helped to understand the situation, matters haven't changed much between the girls. We have alerted the teacher to the situation, and encouraged our daughter to seek other playmates. She's made the adjustment, but my wife and I were disappointed at the hostility the other mother showed us, and her unwillingness to hold her own daughter accountable. Dear Lord, help me to feel (and demonstrate) compassion for this family, even if they do not respond in kind, and even as I am an advocate for my child. Please help me to proceed with grace.

MARCH 23

And forgive us our debts, as we forgive our debtors.

—Matthew 6:12

In quarrels with family members or friends, I am usually quick to forgive and move on; life is too short for grudges! And yet, one area in which forgiveness does not come so easily for me is a pardon of debt. I recently loaned money to a friend, and he has been almost cavalier about paying me back; though we agreed he would repay me in full by last week, he has not done so. I am surprised at how much the situation bothers me, but it was a considerable sum. I see my friend at work, and these last few days, though he seems unconcerned, I have found myself struggling to stay positive and gracious when we are together. It's uncomfortable to bring up, but I know I must talk with him about the loan. God, please grant me the serenity and wisdom to approach this sensitive matter with grace. Teach me how to forgive my friend if he cannot repay me as quickly or completely as I might have hoped.

MARCH 24

Then came Peter to him, and said, Lord, how oft shall my brother sin against me, and I forgive him? till seven times? Jesus saith unto him, I say not unto thee, Until seven times: but, Until seventy times seven.

—Matthew 18:21–22

My aging parents have required more support in the last year or so, and my brother and I have tried to work together to meet their needs. Most of the time we succeed, but in the past few months, we have started butting heads. Part of our disagreements simply stem from the stress of our current circumstances. Both our parents are very ill and usually conflict occurs when I need to put the needs of my own children first. My brother, who doesn't have a wife or family, doesn't always understand when I need to juggle my caregiving roles. I do the best I can, but I recently found out that my brother has been complaining about me to other family members behind my back. I felt hurt and betrayed. I wish he had come to me to resolve our differences. When I confronted him, we had a heated exchange. I didn't receive an apology, and while I assured him I understood and that we would just move on, I have held bitterness in my heart. That resentment has been eating away at me. Yesterday my wife sat me down. She had guessed at my struggle, and counseled me that if ever there was a time for forgiveness, this was it. My brother and I need one another as we cope with the needs of our parents, and the anger I've been harboring is corrosive to my health and spirit. Dear God, please help me to forgive those who I feel have betrayed me. Please help me move forward with a spirit of grace.

MARCH 25

I can do all things through Christ which strengtheneth me.

—Philippians 4:13

I have always been a social drinker. Shy by nature, having a beer helps me relax and feel more comfortable in social settings. But lately I've noticed that I've begun to rely on a drink to unwind after work, or to gear up for a stressful encounter. When I made the decision to cut back, I was surprised and dismayed to discover how dependent I've become on alcohol to fill an emotional need. I think the best path for me is abstinence. Now that I no longer can rely on alcohol to "take off the edge," each day is a struggle. Lord, please give me the strength to persevere in eschewing alcohol. I know my health and well-being will benefit. I thank you for your grace.

MARCH 26

Therefore if any man be in Christ, he is a new creature: old things are passed away; behold, all things are become new.

—2 Corinthians 5:17

When I was a boy, my favorite uncle used to take me fishing on summer evenings when he was in town. Uncle Will was a truck driver, a job that frequently took him away from his family and friends for days at a time, and he formed some bad habits eating alone on the road. Perhaps not surprisingly, after a number of years of this, my uncle developed diabetes and high blood pressure. Will's doctor warned that his eating habits were going to kill him—a serious wake-up call that prompted some life changes. I still remember the evening my uncle and I were out on the river, hoping to catch a pike but mostly reeling in bluegills; he told me it was through God's grace that he was able to change his ways. "I'm healthier," Uncle Will said when I complimented his weight loss. And then he added something I've never forgotten: "God didn't just help me get better, he transformed me. Not just on the outside. On the inside." Lord, you are there to help us better ourselves, not just externally, but internally. Thank you for being there.

MARCH 27

Although our eyes should always be turned above toward God, sometimes we can do with a reminder of God's work just a little bit closer to home. The faith of others can serve as a reminder or an inspiration to strengthen our own faith. Just as we should provide encouragement to others, we can draw on others to help steady ourselves.

MARCH 28

Thine own friend, and thy father's friend, forsake not; neither go into thy brother's house in the day of thy calamity: for better is a neighbour that is near than a brother far off.

—Proverbs 27:10

MARCH 29

As we pass through the phases of our lives, developing or strengthening parts of our personalities, we lose certain friends along the way. But those who travel with us, sharing our personal journeys, reveling in our private growth, are much more than friends. They are our sisters and brothers in Christ.

MARCH 30

The night is given us to take breath, to pray, to drink deep at the fountain of power. The day, to use the strength which has been given us, to go forth to work with it till the evening.

—Florence Nightingale

MARCH 31

Fear thou not; for I am with thee: be not dismayed; for I am thy God: I will strengthen thee; yea, I will help thee; yea, I will uphold thee with the right hand of my righteousness.

—Isaiah 41:10

Lord, either lighten my burden or strengthen my back.

—Thomas Fuller

APRIL

APRIL 1

Thus saith the Lord, The people which were left of the sword found grace in the wilderness; even Israel, when I went to cause him to rest. The Lord hath appeared of old unto me, saying, Yea, I have loved thee with an everlasting love: therefore with lovingkindness have I drawn thee.

—Jeremiah 31:2–3

Lord, let me not be afraid of the wilderness. Let me not be afraid of unanswered questions, of uncertain paths, of scarcity. Let me trust in you and your loving-kindness, that I will have what I need when I need it. Let me trust in your "daily bread," and not get wound up in worries about the future.

APRIL 2

And Jesus being full of the Holy Ghost returned from Jordan, and was led by the Spirit into the wilderness.

—Luke 4:1

Thank you, God, for this new month. This month brings the first inklings of spring to my area, though the trees are still bare. Lord, this month, empty my heart of distractions. Walk with me to the desert and stay with me there, as you pare away those things that draw me away from you.

APRIL 3

Moreover when ye fast, be not, as the hypocrites, of a sad countenance: for they disfigure their faces, that they may appear unto men to fast. Verily I say unto you, They have their reward.

But thou, when thou fastest, anoint thine head, and wash thy face;

That thou appear not unto men to fast, but unto thy Father which is in secret: and thy Father, which seeth in secret, shall reward thee openly.

—Matthew 6:16–18

APRIL 4

Humble yourselves therefore under the mighty hand of God, that he may exalt you in due time: Casting all your care upon him; for he careth for you.

—1 Peter 5:6–7

APRIL 5

So often, Patient One, we become stifled, leading to boredom and whining when circumstances are not as we would have them. What power there is in seeking things not as they are but as they might be, O God, as the children—and I—learn invaluable truths as close as our own backyard.

APRIL 6

Comfort us, God, when we come to this awesome conclusion: What did not satisfy us when we finally laid hold of it was surely not the thing we were so long in seeking. Yes, comfort us by this recognition: In all our longings, we are only yearning for you.

APRIL 7

The Lord is good unto them that wait for him, to the soul that seeketh him.

—Lamentations 3:25

APRIL 8

God, how much longer must I stay curled up in a ball behind this large stone, seeking protection from the storm that swirls around me? I have watched the weeds bow and bend and still not break against the onslaught of the wind. God, I sense I must bend and bow in the midst of the strong forces that pummel me. Then I will find strength to endure until the morning light comes, when I will stand once again because of your help.

APRIL 9

In the sweat of thy face shalt thou eat bread, till thou return unto the ground; for out of it wast thou taken: for dust thou art, and unto dust shalt thou return.

—Genesis 3:19

APRIL 10

May you find joy and satisfaction in your family life: in building a home and setting up a residence—be blessed! in finding a job and working diligently—be blessed! in taking care of little ones and making friends in the neighborhood—be blessed! in seeking God for all your help and guidance, bringing every care to him, yes, I pray, may you indeed be blessed.

APRIL 11

Therefore also now, saith the Lord, turn ye even to me with all your heart, and with fasting, and with weeping, and with mourning:

And rend your heart, and not your garments, and turn unto the Lord your God: for he is gracious and merciful, slow to anger, and of great kindness, and repenteth him of the evil.

—Joel 2:12–13

APRIL 12

Bless my child, O God, who is...
milk mustaches, snaggletoothed grins,
Let the little children come...
tree climber, sand pile architect, chef, and inventor,
Forbid none of them, even...
neon-haired teen with enough pierced body parts to look like fishing lures in a bass
This child, too, a beloved renegade who makes me smile as well as...
student, cocky and shy, foolish and wise
Seeking my plan, my will by daring to search, dream...
grown-up visionary and doer
Using my gifts to build a new world, a better way.
This is our child, a blessing to us both.
Amen.

APRIL 13

And he said unto them, What manner of communications are these that ye have one to another, as ye walk, and are sad?

—Luke 24:17

Jesus spoke these words to the disciples on the road to Emmaus, when they did not yet recognize him. Sometimes even when we are seeking God, our thoughts seem muddled. We find it difficult to see Jesus present and active in our lives. He seems far away. When we talk to others about our faith, as the disciples spoke to one another, sometimes God's presence becomes clear. How many times, when we look back at confusing times with the benefit of hindsight, do we realize that God was with us!

APRIL 14

Take heed therefore unto yourselves, and to all the flock, over the which the Holy Ghost hath made you overseers, to feed the church of God, which he hath purchased with his own blood.

—Acts 20:28

Lord, I thank you today for the full community of believers. We are not alone in seeking you out, and in worshipping you. Being around other people of faith can renew my own. I pray today for all that call out to you. May our faith flourish.

APRIL 15

Is this grace given . . . that now unto the principalities and powers in heavenly places might be known by the church the manifold wisdom of God.

—Ephesians 3:8, 10

God reveals his wisdom through his church. Somewhere in your neighborhood there is a group of imperfect people meeting together, seeking to know God and understand his word. And he promises to use them to encourage each other in this desire.

The Apostle Paul refers to "the fellowship of the mystery" (verse 9). God builds this fellowship, using the church to proclaim the gospel. The church is his body (Ephesians 1:22–23) and it is his bride (Ephesians 5:31–33). What tender images to describe communities of faith. And what a wonderful promise, that his wisdom is made known by the church.

APRIL 16

Draw nigh to God, and he will draw nigh to you. Cleanse your hands, ye sinners; and purify your hearts, ye double minded.

—James 4:8

Be all in today. Clean up your act. Clean up your thoughts. Draw near to God, boldly and completely. There is no place for second thoughts or tentative commitments. It is all in, all the time: seeking God, depending on his strength, believing his promises. If you do this, God will draw near to you. That's all you really need.

APRIL 17

That was the true Light, which lighteth every man that cometh into the world.

—John 1:9

God knows that as hard as we may try, there are times when we will make human mistakes. Even so, if we trust in him and ask his forgiveness, he will bless us with mercy and peace.

APRIL 18

Judge not, and ye shall not be judged: condemn not, and ye shall not be condemned: forgive, and ye shall be forgiven.

—Luke 6:37

Love and forgiveness walk hand-in-hand. Our relationships with God and others are intertwined in this dynamic.

APRIL 19

Forgiveness is not easy. Often it requires us to become far more than we were before; more mature, more accepting, and more compassionate. But once we forgive and stretch ourselves, we can never go back to being that unforgiving and resentful person we were before. We have been opened up, expanded, and set free.

APRIL 20

Coming together in worship with prayer, song, and psalm makes us expectant people. Here we find what we came seeking: your abiding, ever-present daily love. We leave, blessed with the truth that it goes with us into the rest of our lives.

APRIL 21

Lord, how comforting it is to know that you don't require large numbers of people to come together in order for you to be present. So often it's in the spontaneous coming together of two individuals who turn their hearts toward you that your presence is felt most clearly. Thank you for taking time to meet with us, Lord. May you always feel welcome.

APRIL 22

Lord, our vacation time is coming, and with it will be long stretches of travel with the kids. Help us to plan adequately so the trip will go smoothly. Guard us from petty bickering and turn this trip into an opportunity for happy anticipation, recreation, and learning.

May this time of togetherness bond us more deeply as a family and draw us closer to you, O Lord.

Most of all, surround us with your presence so we may rest in safety on your loving shoulders. Amen.

APRIL 23

For all that is in the world, the lust of the flesh, and the lust of the eyes, and the pride of life, is not of the Father, but is of the world.

—1 John 2:16

I recently had lunch with an old college friend, Dan, who always lifts my spirits when we get together. I was excited to share that we've recently purchased a new car. With my youngest daughter out of college, we enjoy a little more disposable income, and so my wife and I splurged on a vehicle loaded with extras. I could tell my friend was happy for me, but as I returned to the car in conversation again and again, I noticed Dan's eyes starting to glaze over. That gave me pause, and I had enough sense to switch gears. I asked about the mission work Dan will be doing in the coming year. Dan, in turn, asked about my daughter's graduation, and our lunch got back on track. I parted from my friend feeling restored, and thankful I'd caught myself before our time together was soured by too much focus on possessions. Lord, thank you for reminding me that it's okay to enjoy material things, but they are just that—things. Being fixated on belongings is not from God.

APRIL 24

But I will hope continually, and will yet praise thee more and more.

—Psalm 71:14

My old college friend Tom is an artist. He lives in a city near my home, and occasionally he'll have a gallery showing of his work downtown. I always try to make his shows, and we usually also manage to get together for a meal every month or so. His shows are a perfect time for me to compliment his work. But one evening when we were just meeting for dinner, I mentioned how impressed I am by a series of sculptures he's been making from pressed wood. Even though I had already praised that same work at a recent show, the innovative nature of the work has stayed with me, and I wanted to share that. Tom was uplifted by my comment. It turns out he'd had a frustrating day in the studio and my admiration, coming from out of the blue like that, meant a lot to him. The experience reminded me that praise is not a one-time thing—you never know when another person might be struggling, or how much repeating a kind word can mean. God, may I remember to uplift others even as I praise you, again and again.

APRIL 25

The day two people make the decision to join their hearts and lives as one is a day of rejoicing. Thank you, God, for the joy of weddings. Please grant your grace on all married couples!

APRIL 26

When I look in my child's eyes, I see the past—the many limbs of the family tree reaching forward to meet in this unique soul.

When I look in my child's eyes, I see the present—the ability to grab each moment and squeeze out each delicious drop.

When I look in my child's eyes, I see the future—all that she will be, all that she will do.

APRIL 27

I am still moving, God, through storms. By your grace—over rough country, you have carried me; amidst pounding waves, you have held me; beyond the horizon of my longings you have shown me your purposes. Even in this small room, sitting still, I am moving, God. Closer.

APRIL 28

Our relationships with others grow, bloom, and sometimes wilt, merely because their time has come. We don't need to regret these passings, for they are a natural part of the earth's movement. Instead, we can look at them with fond recollection, knowing that spring will soon come.

Just as seasons change, God's grace ensures that every friendship has its purpose and time, with his love remaining constant through every transition.

APRIL 29

No one can look at a pine-tree in winter without knowing that spring will come again in due time.

—Frank Bolles

APRIL 30

Dear God, your love embraces me like the warmth of the sun, and I am filled with light. Your hope enfolds me in arms so strong, I lack for nothing. Your grace fills me with the strength I need to move through this day. For these gifts you give me, of eternal love, eternal peace, and most of all, for eternal friendship, I thank you God.

MAY

MAY 1

The Lord hath done great things for us; whereof we are glad.

—Psalm 126:3

MAY 2

Then shall thy light break forth as the morning, and thine health shall spring forth speedily: and thy righteousness shall go before thee; the glory of the Lord shall be thy reward.

—Isaiah 58:8

Dear Lord,

Someone I love is very sick and I am asking in prayer for a healing. I am afraid and anxious for this person and pray for a quick recovery to strength and wholeness again. I also seek guidance, Lord, in how I might best be able to help this person and be there for the support, comfort and love they need most. I seek to be an angel and offer what I can and not be an extra burden to someone already dealing with stress and worry. Please wrap this person in your arms of love, security and caring and be a beacon of light in a time of darkness so that they might not lose hope. Amen.

MAY 3

Rejoice when I run into problems?
Know trials are good for me?
Things like that aren't easy—
Learning to live patiently.

Growing in grace is a process.
Developing character hurts.
Becoming more Christ-like
in all things
Is an everyday process called work.

But if I have faith it is possible.
Faith knowing God loves and cares—
That all my burdens and trials
He also feels and shares.

MAY 4

I have set the Lord always before me: because he is at my right hand, I shall not be moved.

—Psalm 16:8

MAY 5

Father, there are many events in our lives over which we have no control. However, we do have a choice either to endure trying times or to give up. Remind us that the secret of survival is remembering that our hope is in your fairness, goodness, and justice. When we put our trust in you who cannot fail us, we can remain faithful. Our trust and faithfulness produce the endurance that sees us through the tough times we all face in this life. Please help us to remember. Amen.

MAY 6

But the Lord is faithful, who shall stablish you, and keep you from evil.

—2 Thessalonians 3:3

Those who know God delight in his faithfulness.

MAY 7

O Lord, hear my prayer for all who are in trouble this day. Comfort those who are facing the loss of a loved one. After the wrenching grief, let their lonely hours be filled with fond memories of days gone by. Console those who are passing their days without work. During this time of financial stress, give them energy to make their employment the job of finding new work. Encourage those who are finding it difficult to believe in the future. Let your hope fill their hearts as they recall all your past faithfulness. Strengthen those who are doubting the truth of your existence or the validity of your promises. Bring wise friends into their lives who have long known the reality of your love.

MAY 8

O taste and see that the Lord is good: blessed is the man that trusteth in him.

—Psalm 34:8

MAY 9

Lord, if I were to boil down all the good news in the universe and look to see what I'd ended up with, there would be the eternal realities of your goodness, your love, and your faithfulness. And in this world, I don't have to look far for them—family, food, shelter, clothing, seasons, tides, sun, moon, stars, life, beauty, truth, salvation. And that's just a sampling, a preview of a much longer list. I'm moved to praise you and to tell you how much I love you back.

MAY 10

Human faith lives between two extremes, Lord: It's neither completely blind nor able to see everything. It has plenty of evidence when it steps out and trusts you, but it takes each step with a good many questions still unanswered. It's really quite an adventure, this life of faith. And Lord, I must confess that experiencing your faithfulness over time makes it easier and easier to trust you with the unknown in life. Thank you for your unshakable devotion.

MAY 11

Lord, I know you will show your goodness and faithfulness to me if I just diligently seek you. The problem isn't your willingness to give, but my tendency to try to do everything by myself rather than leaning on and trusting in you. This silly inclination brings me needless stress and wastes precious time. Today I endeavor to lay my needs and troubles at your feet the minute I begin to feel the least bit overwhelmed.

MAY 12

God gave the rainbow as a sign of his promise to never flood the entire earth again. The colors that spread out in spectrum, as sunlight passes through water droplets in the sky, speak of God's faithfulness in keeping his promise to Noah and to all the generations that have followed. Faithfulness marks God's character. It is who he is, through and through. Let every rainbow we see remind us of God's faithful love, and let praise flow from our hearts to the one who always keeps his promises.

MAY 13

Every day I'm exposed to a world whose values don't jibe with yours, Lord. I am in need of constant reminders to not get caught up in notions that money, power, status, and physical appearance are of utmost importance. While the movers and shakers of society endorse such things as necessary for a fulfilling existence, you say that faithfulness to you is where real life is lived out and lasting inner peace is achieved. O Lord, help me when I'm tempted to believe that I can prevail in life by being seen as "strong" in ways that ultimately don't matter to you.

MAY 14

As far as the east is from the west, so far hath he removed our transgressions from us.

—Psalm 103:12

MAY 15

My flesh and my heart faileth: but God is the strength of my heart, and my portion for ever.

—Psalm 73:26

MAY 16

Be kind to your little children, Lord.
Be a gentle teacher, patient with our
weakness and stupidity.
And give us the strength and discernment
to do what you tell us,
and so grow in your likeness. May we all
live in the peace that comes from you.
May we journey towards your city, sailing
through the waters of sin
untouched by the waves, borne serenely
along by the Holy Spirit.
Night and day may we give you praise and
thanks, because you have
shown us that all things belong to you,
and all blessings are gifts from you.
To you, the essence of wisdom, the
foundation of truth, be glory for evermore.

—Clement of Alexandria

MAY 17

Lord, I confess to you,
sadly, my sin;
all I am, I tell to you,
all I have been.
Purge all my sin away,
wash clean my soul
this day;
Lord, make me clean.
Then all is peace and
light this soul within;
thus shall I walk with you,
loved though unseen.
Leaning on you, my God,
guided along the road,
nothing between!

—Horatius Bonar

MAY 18

Being confident of this very thing, that he which hath begun a good work in you will perform it until the day of Jesus Christ.

—Philippians 1:6

MAY 19

O Lord, be gracious unto us; we have waited for thee: be thou their arm every morning, our salvation also in the time of trouble.

—Isaiah 33:2

MAY 20

God's grace is our comfort in times of trouble and our beacon of hope amid the blackness of despair. By opening ourselves to God's ever-present grace, we know we are loved and cared for, and our hearts sing out in joyful gratitude.

MAY 21

Jesus Christ the same yesterday, and to day, and for ever.

—Hebrews 13:8

MAY 22

A Lullaby
Amazing Grace,
a mother's face,
a gentle, loving sight.
Arms wrapped like wings,
this angel sings,
a voice so clear and bright.
I rest my soul
basked in the glow
of her protective light.
Amazing Grace,
a peaceful place.
A lullaby goodnight.

MAY 23

And I give unto them eternal life; and they shall never perish, neither shall any man pluck them out of my hand.

—John 10:28

MAY 24

Come, Thou long-expected Jesus,
Born to set thy people free;
From our fears and sin release us;
Let us find our rest in thee.

—Charles Wesley

MAY 25

Christ, the blessed one, gives to all
Wonderful words of life;
Sinner heed now his loving call,
Wonderful words of life.
All so freely given,
Wooing us to heaven:
Beautiful words, wonderful words
Wonderful words of life.

—Philip P. Bliss

MAY 26

Love thou thy fellow man!
He may have sinned, One proof indeed,
He is thy fellow, reach thy hand
And help him in his need!
Love thou thy fellow man. He may
Have wronged thee—then, the less excuse.
Thou hast for wronging him. Obey
What he has dared refuse!
Love thou thy fellow man—for, be
His life a light or heavy load,
No less he needs the love of thee
To help him on his road.

—James Whitcomb Riley

MAY 27

Sometimes I'm like Peter,
and I walk on water.
I stand above my circumstances,
which are like the swirling tempests of the sea.
But then, like Peter,
I take my eyes off Jesus
and concentrate on things below.
Soon I start to sink.
How I long to have
a consistent
water-walking
eyes-on-Jesus faith.

MAY 28

*Let your light so shine before men,
that they may see your good works,
and glorify your Father which
is in heaven.*

—Matthew 5:16

MAY 29

The Lord hath spoken peace to my soul,
He hath blessed me abundantly,
Hath pardoned my sins;
He hath shown me great mercy and saved me by his love.
I will sing of his goodness and mercy while I live,
And ever, forever will praise his holy name.
O how sweet to trust in God,
And to know your sins forgiven,
To believe his precious word,
And be guided by his love.
Therefore goodness and mercy,
Shall follow me all the days of my life. Amen.

—C.E. Leslie

MAY 30

One of the principle rules of religion is to lose no occasion of serving God. And since he is invisible to our eyes, we are to serve him in our neighbor, which he receives as if done to himself in person, standing visibly before us.

—John Wesley

MAY 31

God, when things go wrong, we usually blame you first. Forgive us for even considering that you would deliberately hurt one of your very own children. What could you possibly have to gain? Thank you for your presence, and please forgive our many sins.

JUNE

JUNE 1

I will both lay me down in peace, and sleep: for thou, Lord, only makest me dwell in safety.

—Psalm 4:8

JUNE 2

It's been days since I even considered that I didn't have to be doing all I do alone—pretending to be supermom. Whew! What a relief to know that God remembered and reminded me. Partnerships are so much better than going it alone.

JUNE 3

Since thou wast precious in my sight, thou hast been honourable, and I have loved thee: therefore will I give men for thee, and people for thy life.

—Isaiah 43:4

JUNE 4

Joyful, joyful, we adore thee, God of glory, Lord of love;
hearts unfold like flow'rs before thee,
op'ning to the sun above.
Melt the clouds of sin and sadness,
drive the dark of doubt away;
giver of immortal gladness, fill us with the light of day.
All thy works with joy surround thee,
earth and heav'n reflect thy rays,
stars and angels sing around thee,
center of unbroken praise.
Field and forest, vale and mountain,
flowery meadow, flashing sea,
chanting bird and flowing fountain,
call us to rejoice in thee.

—Henry van Dyke

JUNE 5

Heaven is not reached at a single bound;
But we build the ladder by which we rise
From the lowly earth to the vaulted skies,
And we mount to its summit round by round.

—Josiah Gilbert Holland

JUNE 6

Cast thy burden upon the Lord, and he shall sustain thee: he shall never suffer the righteous to be moved.

—Psalm 55:22

JUNE 7

Hope flies on wings like angels' wings. Hope sings no matter the darkness or the light. Hope lives on when we have the faith that we can believe good things for and from ourselves.

JUNE 8

And Jesus said unto them, I am the bread of life: he that cometh to me shall never hunger; and he that believeth on me shall never thirst.

—John 6:35

JUNE 9

Wings of light surround me,
And I am enlightened.
Wings of love enfold me,
And I am comforted.
Angels guide my journey,
And I am directed.
Angels keep me safe from harm,
And I am protected.
Arms so strong lift me,
And I am emboldened.
Arms so soft hold me,
And I am at peace.
Angels grant me mercy,
And I am redeemed.
Angels walk beside me,
And I am esteemed.
Songs of joy fill me,
And I am enchanted.
Songs of love envelop me,
And I am empowered.
Angels sing above me,
And I am adored.
Angels chant in glory,
And I am restored.

JUNE 10

It is my joy in life to find
At every turning of the road
The strong arm of a comrade kind
To help me onward with my load.
And since I have no gold to give,
And love alone must make amends,
My only prayer is, while I live—
God make me worthy of my friends.

—Frank Dempster Sherman

JUNE 11

If one perfect day was created by me,
These are the things I would most want to see:
Sun in the morning and moonbeams at night,
Birds singing sweetly, then fluttering from sight,
The whispering wind as it passes my face,
The fragrance of baking so sweet to the taste,
Blossoming flowers with shimmering dew,
The sound of the brook as the water roars through,
A kiss from the people that love me the most,
Tender embraces that snuggle me close,
Smiles from kind strangers just walking by,
The sound of a new born babe's gurgles and sighs,
Proud eyes of a grandmother walking with grace,
An old man with memories that show in his face,
My angel that watches and guards from above,
The laughter of children and, mostly, their love.

JUNE 12

Not that we are sufficient of ourselves to think any thing as of ourselves; but our sufficiency is of God.

—2 Corinthians 3:5

JUNE 13

Lord, I believe a rest remains,
To all Thy people known;
A rest where pure enjoyment reigns
And thou art loved alone;
A rest where all our soul's desire
Is fixed on things above;
where fear and sin and grief expire,
Cast out by perfect love.

—Charles Wesley

JUNE 14

If your body suffers pain, and your health you can't regain, and your soul is almost sinking in despair, Jesus knows the pain you feel, he can save and he can heal, take your burden to the Lord and leave it there.

—Charles Albert Tindley

JUNE 15

God, you are invisible but not unseen. You reveal yourself in creation and demonstrate your kindness in a stranger's sincere smile. You are intangible but not unfelt. You caress our faces with the wind and embrace us in a friend's arms. We look for you and feel your presence. Amen.

JUNE 16

God is everything to us and his creation. He is our breath and our life. He is that which makes the sun to rise and the birds to sing. When we call out to God and open ourselves to him, we invite life itself to perch on our shoulder.

JUNE 17

Lord, bless all those today who need healing of any kind. Whether it be physical, emotional, or mental, bless them with your merciful grace and eternal love. Let each one know that they are special in your eyes and that, in the realm of spirit, there is only perfection, wholeness, and joy. Amen.

JUNE 18

And the Lord, he it is that doth go before thee; he will be with thee, he will not fail thee, neither forsake thee: fear not, neither be dismayed.

—Deuteronomy 31:8

JUNE 19

Angel voices, ever singing
Round Thy throne of light,
Angel harps, forever ringing,
Rest not day nor night.

—Francis Pott

JUNE 20

Enter into his gates with thanksgiving, and into his courts with praise: be thankful unto him, and bless his name.

—Psalm 100:4

Sincere gratitude for the gift of life evokes sincere praise.

JUNE 21

He that covereth his sins shall not prosper: but whoso confesseth and forsaketh them shall have mercy.

—Proverbs 28:13

Those who enjoy God's mercy will sing forever.

JUNE 22

O praise the Lord, all ye nations: praise him, all ye people.
For his merciful kindness is great toward us: and the truth of the Lord endureth for ever. Praise ye the Lord.

—Psalm 117:1–2

There's always a reason to sing joyfully.

JUNE 23

Spirit, help me live one day at a time so that I may meet each day's challenges with grace, courage, and hope. Shelter me from the fears of the future and the anguish of the past. Keep my mind and heart focused on the present, where the true gift of happiness and healing is to be found. Amen.

JUNE 24

Over my head—I hear music in the air...
Over my head—I hear singing in the air...
There must be a God somewhere.

—Traditional spiritual

JUNE 27

If I have wounded any soul today,
If I have caused one foot to go astray,
If I have walked in my own willful way,
Dear Lord, forgive!
If I have uttered idle words or vain,
If I have turned aside from want or pain,
Lest I myself shall suffer through the strain,
Dear Lord, forgive!
Forgive the sins I have confessed to Thee;
Forgive the secret sins I do not see;
O guide me, love me and my keeper be,
Dear Lord, Amen.

—C. Maude Battersby

JUNE 28

Teaching them to observe all things whatsoever I have commanded you: and, lo, I am with you always, even unto the end of the world. Amen.

—Matthew 28:20

JUNE 29

God,
You said we should, "Forgive us our sins as we forgive those who sin against us."
Do you realize how hard that can be?
When I've been hurt, my anger and resentment feels justified.
Yet I know that my lack of forgiveness hurts me as much as it hurts the one who hurt me.
I need your help with forgiveness.
Help me forgive anyone who has ever wounded me, however slight or great the hurt.
Forgive me both the offenses I did on purpose and the ways I hurt others without realizing it.
Whenever possible, let me know hot to make amends to those I have hurt.
Help me accept forgiveness from others and graciously offer my own forgiveness. From now on, guide me in a way of living that respects other people and seeks to understand rather than to condemn their actions.
For this is the way that leads to life. Amen.

JUNE 30

Blessed is he whose transgression is forgiven, whose sin is covered.

—Psalm 32:1

JULY

JULY 1

The Lord is nigh unto all them that call upon him, to all that call upon him in truth.

—Psalm 145:18

Some people feel guilty for resorting to prayers of desperation. But God never turns away anyone who sincerely turns to him for help. Even when we've been distant, not walking close to him, he doesn't despise our cries for help as we look to get in step with him again.

JULY 2

And be not conformed to this world: but be ye transformed by the renewing of your mind, that ye may prove what is that good, and acceptable, and perfect, will of God.

—Romans 12:2

This would be a great verse to hang over my bathroom mirror, Lord! As I work on my outward appearance each morning, help me to remember that my inner person needs attention too—especially since that's what you focus on. Your evaluation of my heart is far more important to me than any human opinion about my appearance or fashion sense.

JULY 3

Why do some see you as an angry God, eager to squash us when we sin? Could it be that you've been misrepresented by some who have claimed to represent you? Perhaps. But maybe at times I myself have clung to such wrong notions about you when others have offended me. I paint you with a human brush with such thoughts as, If I were in God's shoes, dealing with that jerk, I'd let that person have it. But when I gather myself, I realize you see each of us as the beautiful being you intended; our failings may bring you sadness, but not hatred. Your perfection is made up not only of absolute holiness, but also of deep mercy. And how I need that mercy every day!

JULY 4

Stand fast therefore in the liberty wherewith Christ hath made us free, and be not entangled again with the yoke of bondage.

—Galatians 5:1

In every human breast, God has implanted a principle, which we call love of freedom; it is impatient of oppression and pants for deliverance.

—Phillis Wheatley

JULY 5

The flowers appear on the earth; the time of the singing of birds is come, and the voice of the turtle is heard in our land.

—Song of Solomon 2:12

Summer begins with a swoop and a splash, like angels scattering on the wind for the ride of their lives.

JULY 6

Thou wilt shew me the path of life: in thy presence is fulness of joy; at thy right hand there are pleasures for evermore.

—Psalm 16:11

On gossamer wings they move as gentle breezes on a warm summer's eve, quietly reminding us that we are always being watched over, always being loved.

JULY 7

When thou passest through the waters, I will be with thee; and through the rivers, they shall not overflow thee: when thou walkest through the fire, thou shalt not be burned; neither shall the flame kindle upon thee.

—Isaiah 43:2

May you always walk with the morning star to guide you, the summer sun on your back, and an angel by your side.

JULY 8

Who sprinkles each bright summer
flower with dew?
Who creates a sunny sensation,
warming all creations?
Who paints the summer skies, reflecting
every shade of blue?
And when autumn comes, who tells the
trees to change their clothes?
Who changes the leaves and instead
drapes the forest in orange and red?
Who designs such beauty? It's the
angels, I suppose.
Who flings a million stars across a
winter sky?
Who tells the northern winds to blow
and covers every hill with snow?
It's the angels working their magic for
the likes of you and I.
And who is assigned in spring to start
the awakening and rebirth?
Who causes the plants to grow and the
whole world to glow?
It's the angels showing off their
handiwork on earth.

JULY 9

Thank heaven for summer rain!
Through the pall of the sweltering sky,
It falls like kisses to the earth,
Renewing and nourishing.
Like a child
I run—
Arms open,
Face to the clouds,
Into the downpour.
All around the people hide
Under doorways and umbrellas,
While the rain pours down on me,
Washing away my gloom.

JULY 10

And we have known and believed the love that God hath to us. God is love; and he that dwelleth in love dwelleth in God, and God in him.

—1 John 4:16

Through it all the angels dance,
Falling leaves and blooming flowers,
Summer's heat and winter's hours,
The ebb and flow of life.
Through it all the angels dance,
Inviting us to dance along,
Or at least to know the song,
Each season of our lives.

JULY 11

Loving God, help us sense your angelic messengers whenever and wherever and however they come to us. In the darkness of winter, the brightness of spring, the abundance of summer, the transitions of autumn, may we expect to be visited by your heavenly beings. And when those visits happen, may our eyes be open and our gratitude heartfelt.

JULY 12

Likewise, I say unto you, there is joy in the presence of the angels of God over one sinner that repenteth.

—Luke 15:10

Angels speak to us in the notes of a hymn, in the soft breezes of summer, in the voice of a child. We need but listen.

JULY 13

Lord, how reassuring it is for me and my children to know something in the world is constant. You send the seasons in your perfect timing, and summer has arrived on schedule. I thank you for this season of warmth and relaxation. It is good to see my children enjoy freedom from the cares and pressures of the school year.

Please guard and protect them through these months, and use this time to restore their energy and enthusiasm to meet the demands of the coming school year.

Surround us all with the beauty of earth's summer wardrobe, and accept our gratitude for the friendliest season of all.

JULY 14

But God commendeth his love toward us, in that, while we were yet sinners, Christ died for us.

—Romans 5:8

To receive grace means that we are given good things in this life, such as angels, whether we deserve them or not.

JULY 15

And he said unto them, Why are ye so fearful? how is it that ye have no faith?

—Mark 4:40

When will the rain let up, Lord? Oh,
soon: may your presence be to me
as cleansing droplets of mercy, these
clouds only filtering in glorious gold and
purple the blazing rays of your grace.

JULY 16

Ask, and it shall be given you; seek, and ye shall find; knock, and it shall be opened unto you.

—Matthew 7:7

God, bless this situation with the gentle, healing power of your love, that I may find the courage to carry on through this dark time of loss and the grace to believe there is happiness ahead. Amen.

JULY 17

Hear counsel, and receive instruction, that thou mayest be wise in thy latter end.

—Proverbs 19:20

Lord, we don't like to let stress destroy our even keel, but sometimes it does. We need your wisdom to help us manage the load and your grace to keep us from being ill-tempered.

JULY 18

But the wisdom that is from above is first pure, then peaceable, gentle, and easy to be intreated, full of mercy and good fruits, without partiality, and without hypocrisy.

—James 3:17

When a long-term relationship comes to an end, it's natural to mourn the loss of a companion and to grieve the death of a particular way of life. But we can mourn and grieve only for so long, then we must ask God to give us the grace and the courage to finally close that door and walk toward a new door waiting to be opened. We must take the next step God has for us.

JULY 19

Abide with me,
fast falls the eventide;
The darkness deepens;
Lord, with me abide!
When other helpers fail
And comforts flee,
Help of the helpless,
O abide with me.
I need thy presence
Every passing hour;
What but thy grace
Can foil the tempter's power?
Who like thyself,
My guide and stay can be?
Through cloud and sunshine,
Lord, abide, with me.

—Henry F. Lyte

JULY 20

Take this burden from me, Lord,
Free me from this pain.
Let me move with ease and grace
And walk in health again.
Take this yoke upon you, Lord,
And help me toward my goal,
I'm tired of being sick and tired
And long to be made whole.
Release me from my illness
And restore me to my best.
If you can do that for me, Lord,
I'll take care of the rest.

JULY 21

My sheep hear my voice, and I know them, and they follow me.

—John 10:27

Children sitting at your knee, Great Teacher, we're collecting footnotes of faith wisdom: In prayer, grumbling is good; in stress, grieving is essential; and in trouble, redeeming grace is promised. In that truth, we'll not drudge through life but rather fly like skiers down a powdery slope.

JULY 22

And God is able to make all grace abound toward you; that ye, always having all sufficiency in all things, may abound to every good work.

—2 Corinthians 9:8

We are blessed as we remember God's grace.

JULY 23

Father God, we know that to receive the blessing of healing, the heart must be open. But when we are mad, we close off the heart as if it were a prison. Remind us that a heart that is shut cannot receive understanding, acceptance, and renewal. Even though we feel angry, we must keep the heart's door slightly ajar so your grace can enter and fill our darkness with the light of hope.

JULY 24

Let us therefore desire nothing else, wish for nothing else, and let nothing please and delight us except our Creator and Redeemer, and Savior, the only true God, who is full of good, who alone is good, and from whom, and through whom, and in whom is all mercy, all grace, all glory of all penitents and of the just, and of all the blessed rejoicing in heaven.

—St. Francis of Assisi

Lord, teach me how to help and defend the vulnerable people around me—the children, the sick, the infirm, the elderly, the poor. They are easily taken advantage of by those more powerful than they are, but I know you have a special place in your heart for them. Grant me your wisdom, insight, and grace to effectively help wherever and whenever I can.

JULY 25

God,
Not a day goes by, dear God, when your faith in me doesn't show up as some small miracle in my life. I am in awe of your belief in me, even when I don't believe in myself. Your loving grace gives me the courage to do anything, and your trust in me strengthens my resolve. I am so grateful you see me through the eyes of a loving Father, and you never let me down or abandon me in my times of need. Thank you, God, for the faith that can move mountains, and for helping me to realize that with you beside me, all those mountains are nothing more than large hills that can be easily climbed. I cherish your faith in me, God. Amen.

JULY 26

For all things are for your sakes, that the abundant grace might through the thanksgiving of many redound to the glory of God.

—2 Corinthians 4:15

Dear Lord,
How often do I ask you for things, and rarely say thank you? I pray today only to say thanks for the continued miracles and blessings, big and small, that make up my life each day. I want to thank you for your presence, which I know I can always count on, and for your love, which never wanes or lets me down. I want to thank you for your mercy, and for your forgiveness, even though I am sure there are times I don't deserve it. Living in your grace each day, Lord, is an exercise in continuous gratitude, and even when life challenges me or throws me a curveball, you are there at the ready with guidance and strength. For this and so much more, I thank you, Lord. Amen.

JULY 27

If my people, which are called by my name, shall humble themselves, and pray, and seek my face, and turn from their wicked ways; then will I hear from heaven, and will forgive their sin, and will heal their land.

—2 Chronicles 7:14

Truly, forgiveness is a healing gift from above.

JULY 28

I became enchanted
By my angel when I felt
The touch of silken fingers
Brush my face so tenderly.
I became empowered
By my angel when I heard
Loving, caring whispers
Of forgiveness to my soul.
I became protected
By my angel when I saw
The sanctuary of her wings
And a soft cocoon of light.
I became enlightened
By my angel when I found
My dreams in stars that I could reach,
Sparkling inside of me.

JULY 29

Repent ye therefore, and be converted, that your sins may be blotted out, when the times of refreshing shall come from the presence of the Lord.

—Acts 3:19

I pray, Lord, for the ability to learn forgiveness. Often within my heart there is much that is negative. I pray to learn to let go of those feelings. I pray to learn to forgive others as I wish to be forgiven. I pray for the gifts of understanding and compassion as I strive to be more like you. Amen.

JULY 30

And when ye stand praying, forgive, if ye have ought against any: that your Father also which is in heaven may forgive you your trespasses.

—Mark 11:25

We're stained, like a paint rag, by troubles we caused ourselves, Lord. Red, the color of lost temper and rudeness. Green, envy of others who have it easier and more of it. Blue, the shade of despair over something we could change. Yellow, of cowardly running. Rearrange our unsightly smudges into glorious rainbows through your gift of forgiveness.

JULY 31

Lord, it is tempting and easy to cast a scornful eye on those around us and note every fault. When my pride tempts me to do so, prompt me to turn the magnifying glass on myself instead. If I keep in mind how much I need your forgiveness every day, my love for you will never grow cold. I know you are willing to forgive each and every fault if I only ask.

AUGUST

AUGUST 1

Will there always be poor people among us? Yes. God's Word says as much, but it's not in the context of hopelessness. It's in the context of a command for us to be generous. And it's a very beautiful picture, really, of the heart of God toward all humanity. Our tangible gifts to help the poor mirror God's spiritual gifts that keep flowing toward us to meet our needs. As our hands extend food, clothing, and shelter to those who lack it, God's hands extend grace, mercy, and forgiveness to give us all that our needy souls lack.

AUGUST 2

Lord, sometimes my past rises up to haunt me—or worse yet, to bite me. These are the real-world consequences of poor choices I've made. But even though I'm reminded of them because of the cause-and-effect nature of things, once I confess them to you and receive your forgiveness, they are erased from your record book. So even when I'm reminded of my old sins in one way or another, help me to quickly let go of any guilt or shame that rears its ugly head. While consequences may linger, your forgiveness is complete. Thank you for that eternal reality.

AUGUST 3

A wise friend once gave me some advice I have come back to again and again over the course of my life. I was having trouble getting past some mistakes I had made, and my friend advised me to ask myself, "Am I feeling condemned by the devil, or am I being convicted by God's Spirit?" Condemnation, she told me, is never from God. "The devil will try to make you feel like you're just plain worthless," she said. "The Holy Spirit, by contrast, will direct you to confess your wrongdoing, receive God's forgiveness, make amends where you can, and get going in the right direction."

AUGUST 4

How many times has my anger produced regret, Father? More times than I can count. Thomas Jefferson advised counting to ten when angry and to a hundred when very angry. Too often, though, I'm more prone to Mark Twain's approach: "When angry, count four; when very angry, swear."

But I know that's not okay. I want to take the high road as often as possible. I want to be patient when frustrated, dignified when wronged. I confess my slowness to listen, my quickness to speak, and my habit of letting anger rule the moment. Here is a fresh start right now as I receive your forgiveness. Please lead me forward as one who is focused on following in your footsteps.

AUGUST 5

When I have one foot in the worldly scene and one foot in your kingdom, Lord, I'm compromising. Your ways of humility, love, and forgiveness are so at odds with worldly material values that there is no way to play both fields at once. I have a choice to make. Do I choose to indulge in a lifetime of hedonistic pleasures, or will I choose to serve you, walking in your peaceful ways now and looking forward to the promise of eternity? I know what I choose, Lord. That's why I'm spending time with you right now. Help me to walk without compromise today.

AUGUST 6

Lord, help us to help each other find you. Help us to encourage each other and to not be too sensitive to constructive criticism. For my part, I ask your forgiveness for all the times I have willingly polluted my mind and spirit by choosing a questionable form of entertainment over a more life-affirming one. Protect me from destructive habits, Lord. I know there are better ways to spend my precious moments on this earth.

AUGUST 7

Take my hand, precious Lord, as I take on the role of peacemaker. Lead me through the minefield of broken relationships between my child and another.

Make me sensitive to hurt feelings on both sides, and fill me with the compassion and understanding to negotiate the delicate situation fairly.

Give both children an appreciation for the friendship they have enjoyed, and make them understand the need for apology and forgiveness. Help them to put the past behind them, start fresh, and build a new relationship.

It is painful to see misery on these young children's faces, Lord. Use me to help them mend this friendship and restore the sunshine.

AUGUST 8

Father, you are a God of love, compassion, and forgiveness. You have shown my family the right way to live in the world. You are a God my children can rely on to guide them and keep safe. What wonders you perform!

Your power at work in us can accomplish more than our meager minds can even conceive. You boost our confidence and make us better than we are.

In times of trouble, you find solutions we never could have imagined. Lord, we do not deserve your care and attention, but you give them anyway. For this we exalt you forever.

AUGUST 9

Dear Lord, life can easily become too serious when motherly responsibilities overwhelm me. As I deal with my children each day, let me not forget my sense of humor. Humor can soothe ruffled feelings, calm tempers, and lighten our moods when we become too somber.

Laughter can diffuse tension, chase away anger, and make forgiveness easier. It's even good for our health.

Lord, I thank you for your healing gift of humor. Grant to my children, also, the ability to enjoy the humorous side of life and receive all of its benefits.

AUGUST 10

Loving God, sometimes when my children and I have a difference of opinion, they translate that difference as a lack of care for them. Everything I do is for them. How can I convince them that I am on their side—that my opposition to their opinions or actions grows out of my love and concern for them?

I want my children to know that my love, my help, my forgiveness, are there for the taking; that I am always ready to listen to and comfort them.

Lord, your great love has at times been misunderstood and misinterpreted by your children. You have been down this same road. Help me to demonstrate that I care. Let my love penetrate the walls that go up between me and my children, just as your love has done when I've turned away from you.

AUGUST 11

Father, how do I guard my children against being selfish and always wanting their own way? At times I can't believe these are my offspring. I have treated them with love and respect, yet they persist in their stubbornness. Is this just a phase? Have I given too much and not expected enough of them?

Is this a reflection of myself when I rebel against you, Lord? You give me everything I need, yet often I insist on "doing my own thing." But you always draw me back to your loving arms, to seek your forgiveness and your wisdom. Draw my children back, O Lord, to the circle of your love.

AUGUST 12

Father, it is important to us that our children be honest with us and not try to deceive us. We have brought up all of our children to love you, Lord. We want each of them to develop a godly character, fit for a child of the King.

Walk with us and guide us as we encourage our children to be truthful. Keep the lines of communication open between us so they won't feel the need for falsehood. When a lapse occurs, put forgiveness in our hearts so we can put the incident behind us and help our children walk in truth once more.

AUGUST 13

Be it known unto you therefore, men and brethren, that through this man is preached unto you the forgiveness of sins and by him all that believe are justified from all things, from which ye could not be justified by the law of Moses.

—Acts 13:38–39

God,

I ask in prayer for your forgiveness. I've not been the most loving and kind person lately, and I've treated people terribly as a result. I plan to reach out to each and every one of them and ask their forgiveness, but first I come to you in hopes that you will help me be a better person, a more loving and caring friend, and someone who treats others as I'd like to be treated. Please take away the defects in me that cause me to do harm to others, and strengthen the good qualities I have. I am a loving person, but when life backs me into a corner, I know I can be awful. Please forgive me and empower me to make better choices in the future and be the person you want me to be. Amen.

AUGUST 14

Giving thanks unto the Father, which hath made us meet to be partakers of the inheritance of the saints in light:

Who hath delivered us from the power of darkness, and hath translated us into the kingdom of his dear Son:

In whom we have redemption through his blood, even the forgiveness of sins.

—Colossians 1:12–14

AUGUST 15

He will turn again, he will have compassion upon us; he will subdue our iniquities; and thou wilt cast all their sins into the depths of the sea.

—Micah 7:19

I need to ask someone for forgiveness. Part of me wants to brush off and minimize what I did, to say that what I did wasn't so bad—maybe the other person didn't even notice! But I don't want to start to walk astray in little things. God, give me strength to do this properly and offer a genuine, loving apology.

AUGUST 16

Husbands, love your wives, even as Christ also loved the church, and gave himself for it.

—Ephesians 5:25

Almighty God, I honestly don't know how a marriage survives without forgiveness. In fact, maybe the marriages without it don't survive. Thank you for a forgiving wife, Lord. Because she forgives me so often, it's much easier for me to forgive her when she does something thoughtless. Forgiveness prevents the weeds from taking root in a relationship and provides an environment where love can grow. Bless our marriage, Lord, and keep it well watered with forgiveness.

AUGUST 17

This is my commandment, That ye love one another, as I have loved you.

—John 15:12

Angels skip along the seashore picking up shells, kissing each one, and whispering, "Good job!" Angels traipse through the galaxy, touching stars and dancing on planets. Angels waltz through the heavens, full of joy and worship, flowing with majesty, rhythm, and love.

AUGUST 18

And above all things have fervent charity among yourselves: for charity shall cover the multitude of sins.

—1 Peter 4:8

What know we of the Blest above
But that they sing, and that they love?

—William Wordsworth

AUGUST 19

Cause me to hear thy lovingkindness in the morning; for in thee do I trust: cause me to know the way wherein I should walk; for I lift up my soul unto thee.

—Psalm 143:8

I think that the purpose and cause of the Incarnation [the coming of Jesus] was that God might illuminate the world by his wisdom and excite it to the love of himself.

—Peter Abelard

AUGUST 20

The Lord is not slack concerning his promise, as some men count slackness; but is longsuffering to us-ward, not willing that any should perish, but that all should come to repentance.

—2 Peter 3:9

Lord, perfect for me what is lacking of thy gifts; of faith, help thou mine unbelief; of hope, establish my trembling hope; of love, kindle its smoking flax.

—Lancelot Andrewes

AUGUST 21

Under his wings I am safely abiding,
though the night deepens and tempests are wild;
still I can trust him, I know he
will keep me,
he has redeemed me and I am his child.
Under his wings, under his wings, who
from his love can sever?
Under his wings my soul shall abide,
safely abide forever.
Under his wings, O what precious enjoyment!
There will I hide till life's trials are o'er;
sheltered, protected,
no evil can harm me,
resting in Jesus I'm safe evermore.
Under his wings, under his wings, who
from his love can sever?
Under his wings my soul shall abide,
safely abide forever.
—William O. Cushing

AUGUST 22

Therefore, my beloved brethren, be ye stedfast, unmoveable, always abounding in the work of the Lord, forasmuch as ye know that your labour is not in vain in the Lord.

—1 Corinthians 15:58

Lord, you are here,
Lord, you are there.
You are wherever we go.
Lord, you guide us,
Lord, you protect us.
You are wherever we go.
Lord, we need you,
Lord, we trust you,
You are wherever we go.
Lord, we love you,
Lord, we praise you,
You are wherever we go.

AUGUST 23

Be careful for nothing; but in every thing by prayer and supplication with thanksgiving let your requests be made known unto God. And the peace of God, which passeth all understanding, shall keep your hearts and minds through Christ Jesus.

—Philippians 4:6-7

Lord, dismiss us with thy blessing,
Hope, and comfort from above;
Let us each, thy peace possessing,
Triumph in redeeming love.

—Robert Hawker

AUGUST 24

These Blessings, Reader,
may Heav'n grant to thee;
A faithful Friend, equal in Love's degree;
Land fruitful, never conscious of the Curse,
A liberal Heart and never-failing Purse;
A smiling Conscience, a contented mind;
A temp'rate Knowledge with true
Wisdom join'd;
A Life as long as fair, and when expir'd,
A kindly Death, unfear'd as undesire'd.
—Ben Franklin

AUGUST 25

The Lord thy God in the midst of thee is mighty; he will save, he will rejoice over thee with joy; he will rest in his love, he will joy over thee with singing.

—Zephaniah 3:17

Four stages of growth in Christian maturity

Love of self for self's sake

Love of God for self's sake

Love of God for God's sake

Love of self for God's sake.

—St. Bernard of Clairvaux

AUGUST 26

Lord, you know better than I know myself that I am growing older, and will some day be old....

Release me from craving to straighten out everybody's affairs.... With my vast store of wisdom it seems a pity not to use it all, but you know that I want a few friends at the end.

....seal my lips on my own aches and pains—they are increasing, and my love of rehearsing this is becoming sweeter as the years go by....

Keep me reasonably sweet. I do not want to be a saint—some of them are so hard to live with—but a sour old woman is one of the crowning works of the devil.

—Anonymous

AUGUST 27

I will lift up mine eyes unto the hills, from whence cometh my help.

—Psalm 121:1

Yet, in the maddening maze of things,
And tossed by storm and flood,
To one fixed trust my spirit clings;
I know that God is good!...
I know not where His islands lift
Their fronded palms in air;
I only know I cannot drift
Beyond His love and care.

—John Greenleaf Whittier, "The Eternal Goodness"

AUGUST 28

Love is greater than faith, because the end is greater than the means. What is the use of having faith? It is to connect the soul to God. And what is the object of connecting man with God? That he may become like God. But God is Love. Hence, Faith, the means, is in order to Love, the end. Love, therefore, obviously is greater than faith. 'If I have all faith, so as to remove mountains, but have not love, I am nothing.'

—Henry Drummond

AUGUST 29

He that loveth not knoweth not God;
for God is love.

—1 John 4:8

God stretches our heart's capacity when he tells us to love our enemies. Loving them proves that we belong to God, for he loves everyone, no matter what they have done.

AUGUST 30

Waiting,
endless waiting.
Why does it seem impossible
to wait patiently
and
graciously—
for the overdue phone call
or the long-expected letter...
for delayed company to arrive
or a sick loved one to get better?
Is there a special ingredient
to fill the waiting time
and ease the heavy burdens
that weigh upon my mind?
Could waiting possibly achieve a work
which nothing else can do?
God, teach me how to
wait patiently
and put full trust
in you.

AUGUST 31

Skipping up the sidewalk . . . first day of school. Reading, writing, 'rithmetic. First steps, first dates, first jobs. Hurrying down the sidewalk, diploma in hand . . . last day of school. What more can I say, dear God, than I've said since before my beloved graduate was born? Watch over and visit this young person with your presence. We've done a pretty good job so far, you and I. And now it's time to let go. Be with me. I'm better at roots than wings. Remind me that nothing can separate us from one another or your love. Help me be there for my children as you are for me, companion God. Go with this child today. I mustn't follow too closely, and I can't yet judge my distance.

SEPTEMBER

SEPTEMBER 1

But love ye your enemies, and do good, and lend, hoping for nothing again; and your reward shall be great, and ye shall be the children of the Highest: for he is kind unto the unthankful and to the evil.

—Luke 6:35

The kindness of angels has always been available. You invoke it yourself when you show love to another person.

SEPTEMBER 2

Let me be an angel to someone today.
Let me make life easier in some important way.
Let me offer kindness as I go
and cultivate the seeds of hope
so they might bloom and grow.
Let me be a blessing to a stranger or friend.
Let me find a broken heart that I can help to mend.
Let me offer words of love to those who know despair
and tend to wounds of others
with compassion, hope, and care.
Let me be an angel to someone in need.
Let me be the bearer of some unexpected deed.
Let me teach the ways of love to everyone I see
and bring the gift of peace to those
who seek serenity.

SEPTEMBER 3

A lonely widow sits in her rocker;
life seems filled with despair.
But when she reads her scriptures,
she knows that Christ is there.
Children playing on the playground,
one stands alone and no one cares.
Then someone walks up and makes a friend,
and the love of Christ is there.
Three young children and no husband;
the kids seem always in her hair.
She prays when she tucks them into bed at night,
and she knows that Christ is there.
He comes home from work exhausted;
his dear wife helps him to his chair.
A meager meal is hot and ready,
and they're thankful Christ is there.
A car is parked along the highway,
stopped because a tire has no air.
Someone stops to lend a helping hand,
and it's clear that Christ is there.
To the widowed and the fatherless,
or the hurting with despair,
reach out to them with kindness in your heart
and let them know that Christ is there.
If this seems just all too much to take,
and you feel life isn't fair,
just think of and empty cross and tomb,
and remember—Christ was there.

SEPTEMBER 4

But and if ye suffer for righteousness' sake, happy are ye: and be not afraid of their terror, neither be troubled.

—1 Peter 3:14

Father,

It's not always clear to me why suffering comes. But it is clear to me that whenever I do suffer, you are close at hand. I can see you in the kindnesses you deliver to me through your angels. Some angels are strangers, some are friends, some are unseen, but all remind me that you see me, that you care for me, that you are with me. Amen

SEPTEMBER 5

Grow in the grace and knowledge of our Lord and Savior Jesus Christ.

—2 Peter 3:18

When you've given all you can,
angels are watching.

When you've returned kindness for
difficulty, angels are standing.

When you've forgiven the
unforgivable, angels are applauding.

When you've suffered, but not lost
yourself, angels are weeping with joy.

SEPTEMBER 6

For God is not unrighteous to forget your work and labour of love, which ye have shewed toward his name, in that ye have ministered to the saints, and do minister.

—Hebrews 6:10

Put on your halo every day to be a blessing to others and to share small kindnesses with those you pass along your way.

SEPTEMBER 7

Put on therefore, as the elect of God, holy and beloved, bowels of mercies, kindness, humbleness of mind, meekness, longsuffering;

Forbearing one another, and forgiving one another, if any man have a quarrel against any: even as Christ forgave you, so also do ye.

And above all these things put on charity, which is the bond of perfectness.

And let the peace of God rule in your hearts, to the which also ye are called in one body; and be ye thankful.

Let the word of Christ dwell in you richly in all wisdom; teaching and admonishing one another in psalms and hymns and spiritual songs, singing with grace in your hearts to the Lord.

And whatsoever ye do in word or deed, do all in the name of the Lord Jesus, giving thanks to God and the Father by him.

—Colossians 3:12–17

SEPTEMBER 8

Lord, I am in urgent need of an extra dose of patience with my children. Sometimes I think I cannot bear another whine, another scream, another temper tantrum. My nerves are worn thin, and I am tempted to react in kind.

How I would like to be able to handle each situation calmly, but I am not perfect, and what I want to do, I cannot do without your help.

Father, guide me daily. You are a God of infinite kindness and patience. Let the waves of your love wash over me. When rough times occur, enable me to keep the children's behavior in perspective, and let me look at their undesirable actions through eyes filtered by your love. Help me deal with them in an effective way, one that is acceptable to you.

SEPTEMBER 9

Lord, why is it that we mothers feel embarrassed when our youngsters misbehave in public? They are just being children, yet our cheeks burn with shame when they are less than perfect. Then, to cover our embarrassment, we treat them unfairly or embarrass them.

Forgive me when I react to my children in a less-than-loving way, Father. You never withhold your love from me. Grant me the wisdom and understanding to deal with problems before they get out of hand; to avoid the anger that clouds my good judgment.

Childhood passes so quickly. I don't want to spend it scolding and reprimanding. Show me how to deal with my children in loving kindness, as you do, and to let them know how much they mean to me.

SEPTEMBER 10

Bless us in this time of good fortune. Give us the grace to be grateful for newfound comforts, magnanimous among those who have less, and thoroughly giving with all we've been given. Amen.

SEPTEMBER 11

God, how often do we feel rejection of some sort? I know the sting of not being loved by someone I was once in love with, or the denial of a dream job, or just feeling as though I cannot do anything right. But you never judge, you never deny, you never reject me. May I also offer my own love without judgment and rejection, and give of it freely to anyone who might be lifted up or healed in some small way by my gesture of kindness and compassion.

SEPTEMBER 12

Submit yourselves therefore to God. Resist the devil, and he will flee from you.

—James 4:7

SEPTEMBER 13

It isn't hard to resist Satan, our ancient foe. All we have to do is submit to God. That's what we struggle with. We often actually want the satisfaction or pleasure of our sin. That's how Satan tempts us in the first place. But if we think about what God would have us do, and then just do it, sin loses its allure. When we consider God's kindness and purpose, when we see his holiness and love, then we can easily submit to him, and the devil runs away.

SEPTEMBER 14

Be not afraid of sudden fear, neither of the desolation of the wicked, when it cometh. For the Lord shall be thy confidence, and shall keep thy foot from being taken.

—Proverbs 3:25–26

It's a scary world, and it's easy to be fearful. But we shouldn't be, not if our confidence is in the sovereign mercy and kindness of our God. The picture here is of a foot caught in a snare, as if someone was hunting for us and trying to capture us. But the writer says the Lord won't let that happen. The Lord will guide our steps and keep us safe. So, be not afraid of sudden fear. Let the Lord be your confidence.

SEPTEMBER 15

He doth execute the judgment of the fatherless and widow, and loveth the stranger, in giving him food and raiment.

—Deuteronomy 10:18

When I was a boy, my Sunday School teacher encouraged us, one week, to keep track of the kind things we did for others. I prepared a careful ledger, describing the dishes I washed for my mom after dinner, the popcorn I shared with my younger brother. The next Sunday, I proudly showed my list to the teacher. "Great job, that is very kind," he praised my efforts. I looked up to this man the way I looked up to my own father. We talked about how important it is to do kindnesses for the ones we love, and then he said, "And the next step, son, is to serve those we don't even know!'" He explained that while it takes just that little bit more effort to extend ourselves for strangers, that is Christ's way. Dear Lord, all these years later, those words have stayed with me; may I be generous to strangers, not just to those I know and love.

SEPTEMBER 16

And God gave Solomon wisdom and understanding exceeding much, and largeness of heart, even as the sand that is on the sea shore.

—1 Kings 4:29

I don't have a lot of money, God, so when I think about giving to others, I often feel as though I have nothing of value to offer. Then I remember the times I sat with my grandparents before they passed away, listening to their stories and experiences, absorbing their wisdom, and cherishing their advice. I realized I have so much to offer to those around me. I have love and life experience and enough wisdom to help those who ask for it. I have a heart full of compassion and understanding. I have kindness. Thank you, God, for the gifts you instilled in me so I could pass them on to others...gifts no amount of money can buy.

SEPTEMBER 17

Yea, the Lord shall give that which is good; and our land shall yield her increase.

—Psalm 85:12

Autumn brings lazy and gradual like the lightest of angels floating down to earth on the back of a wide, mapleleaf magic carpet.

SEPTEMBER 18

When an angel smiles, the sun
shines through the rain.

When an angel smiles, the cool
wind begins to blow.

When an angel smiles, a small
child wakes.

When an angel smiles, a new
flake forms of snow.

When an angel smiles, the first
autumn leaf falls.

When an angel smiles, a
musician writes a song.

When an angel smiles, a young
bird learns to call.

When an angel smiles,
somebody smiles along.

SEPTEMBER 19

Rejoicing in hope; patient in tribulation; continuing instant in prayer.

—Romans 12:12

Maturity: facing each new day with patience, calmness, and confidence that God is in control.

SEPTEMBER 20

Strengthened with all might, according to his glorious power, unto all patience and longsuffering with joyfulness.

—Colossians 1:11

Have courage for the great sorrows of life and patience for the small ones; and when you have laboriously accomplished your daily task, go to sleep in peace. God is awake.

—Victor Hugo

SEPTEMBER 21

And not only so, but we glory in tribulations also: knowing that tribulation worketh patience;

And patience, experience; and experience, hope:

And hope maketh not ashamed; because the love of God is shed abroad in our hearts by the Holy Ghost which is given unto us.

—Romans 5:3–5

Just when all seems hopeless, prayer lifts us like a wave on the ocean. A sturdy craft, prayer doesn't hide from pain, but uses it like the force of the sea to move us to a new place of insight, patience, courage, and sympathy. Always, it is God's hand beneath the surface holding us up.

SEPTEMBER 22

And let us not be weary in well doing: for in due season we shall reap, if we faint not.

—Galatians 6:9

Ask your angel for an added measure of patience when every question asked is a silly one and every one you try to help works against you.

SEPTEMBER 23

Wait on the Lord: be of good courage, and he shall strengthen thine heart: wait, I say, on the Lord.

—Psalm 27:14

Progress, in the folds of a family, O God, is not a straight, flat line but rather ups and downs. Like squiggles on a heart monitor, they merely chart the daily rhythm of life. Give me energy and patience to go with the flow.

SEPTEMBER 24

As one whom his mother comforteth, so will I comfort you; and ye shall be comforted in Jerusalem.

—Isaiah 66:13

A word of advice to mothers of kids who disobey, rebel, and test patience and values: Remain calm but resolute, for kids need the security of boundaries and consequences.

SEPTEMBER 25

Peace I leave with you, my peace I give unto you: not as the world giveth, give I unto you. Let not your heart be troubled, neither let it be afraid.

—John 14:27

Enduring hardship with patience reveals the reality of faith. Godly patience brings peace with others.

SEPTEMBER 26

Likewise, ye younger, submit yourselves unto the elder. Yea, all of you be subject one to another, and be clothed with humility: for God resisteth the proud, and giveth grace to the humble.

—1 Peter 5:5

Everyone we meet is an angel in disguise, even those who vex our spirits and challenge our patience. They, above all, teach us humanity and humility.

SEPTEMBER 27

*This is the day which the Lord hath made;
we will rejoice and be glad in it.*

—Psalm 118:24

You don't have to pass an exam to be an angel, but your patience and your temper will be tested when you least expect it.

SEPTEMBER 28

A friend loveth at all times, and a brother is born for adversity.

—Proverbs 17:17

God has given true friends an abundance of wisdom, patience, and kindness.

SEPTEMBER 29

No matter how hard I try, God of patience and support, someone finds fault with me. I am mortified about the latest criticism. I can't decide whether to run away in shame or storm back and defend my actions, for I thought I was right. Criticism hurts most when coupled with ridicule, and I feel like less of a person for the tone in which I was addressed. Give me the courage to confront this, Lord, for it is not acceptable to be treated this way even when in error. Keep me calm, factual, and open; perhaps the tone was unintentional, the critic unaware of the power of shaming. Help me remember how I feel now the next time I find fault with someone. As I've learned firsthand with you the zillions of times I messed up, there are better ways to confront mistakes than with stinging criticisms that divide and demean. Truth be known, Lord, such abrasive manners say more about the criticizer than the criticized. Keep me from passing them on.

SEPTEMBER 30

Dear God, for our family we ask your love and care in the days and years ahead. We pray for the strength to go to work every day. It's not easy to get up early and then go out to face the world. The competition is tough, the bottom line inflexible. Give us the strength to work.

We pray for the health of each family member. You know our bodies better than we do. Every ache and pain, every sickness, is a concern to you. Therefore we ask that you keep watch over our bones and muscles and every bodily system, because you are the Great Healer. We ask for guidance in all the decisions we must make in the days ahead, the big decisions, and even the little daily ones. We acknowledge that without divine direction, our lives become meaningless, wrapped up in our own selfishness, heading nowhere. Lead us where you want us to go!

OCTOBER

OCTOBER 1

Depart from evil, and do good; seek peace, and pursue it.

—Psalm 34:14

Lord, bring me to the place where peace flows like a river, where soft green grasses gently hold the weight of my tired body, where the light of a new sunrise casts warmth.

OCTOBER 2

Where no counsel is, the people fall: but in the multitude of counsellors there is safety.

—Proverbs 11:14

Lord, I need you here in the midst of this difficult situation, that the very warmth of your love will bring about the resolution and that the brightness of your light will cast out all shadows between us. Amen.

OCTOBER 3

Then thine handmaid said, The word of my lord the king shall now be comfortable: for as an angel of God, so is my lord the king to discern good and bad: therefore the Lord thy God will be with thee.

—2 Samuel 14:17

The presence of an angel is like a snowflake lightly touching you with its special gift, then evaporating into your warmth as you hurry on your way.

OCTOBER 4

Thus the heavens and the earth were finished, and all the host of them.

—Genesis 2:1

Recognizing the presence of angels around you can feel like walking from the shadows into the warmth of sunshine. Suddenly, you feel the nourishment that comes from someone taking the time to look out just for you and you alone.

OCTOBER 5

Why am I so uneasy?
What's this quest I make?
The mystery is fleeting;
This longing's hard to shake.
I'm told there is a warm light
Filled with hope and love,
A light that fills our souls up,
A glow sent from above.
My cluttered mind needs clearing;
Tangled thoughts are tied.
I relax, breathe deep, and wait
For his presence by my side.
The Light of Love I yearn for
Needs only my request
I close my eyes and ask God
For calm and quiet rest.
A stillness soon takes over,
Loosening the bind.
Serenity and God's peace
Have cleared my troubled mind.
Oh, Lord, I feel your presence:
Love and warmth and light.
My troubled soul is open,
And soon my heart feels right.
I bask for just a moment,
In the light of love he gives.
I'm filled with God's assurance,
That YES, my Savior lives.

OCTOBER 6

The sun shall be no more thy light by day; neither for brightness shall the moon give light unto thee: but the Lord shall be unto thee an everlasting light, and thy God thy glory.

—Isaiah 60:19

The light that shines upon me,
The arms that reach to hold me,
The warmth that gives me comfort,
The angel's wings enfold me.
The word that gives me power,
The song that makes me whole,
The wisdom that empowers me,
The touch that heals my soul.

OCTOBER 7

May your eyes look kindly upon this family, Lord, for we need your love and guidance in our lives. This is a family that seeks to do the right things—to work hard for a living, to raise up children who will contribute to society, and to be a blessing in our neighborhood. But we know we need your constant help to do these things. May we be filled with love and happiness—all of us who live in this home: by fulfilling our responsibilities, day in and day out; by being accountable in all our actions; by giving whenever we can, even when it hurts; by nurturing warmth and understanding among us. And by always looking out for the best interests of others. Please grant our requests according to your great goodness.

OCTOBER 8

Be not deceived: evil communications corrupt good manners.

—1 Corinthians 15:33

Today's challenge? Trust in him at all times. When unexpected challenges arise, turn your heart to him instead of you friends on Facebook. Let him be your refuge at all times.

OCTOBER 9

The Lord is my strength and my shield; my heart trusted in him, and I am helped: therefore my heart greatly rejoiceth; and with my song will I praise him.

—Psalm 28:7

Loving God, I have dedicated my children to you and have promised to teach them your laws. Sometimes I feel ineloquent, inadequate, unfit for the task. But you are with me, Lord; you can supply what I lack.

I long to show my loved ones how to walk daily in your light, to bask in your warmth, and to love you with all of their hearts.

Please grant me the understanding I need to show each child how to worship and obey you, so they may experience the joy of your presence in their lives.

Your love fills me with song, O Lord. Help me teach the words to my children.

OCTOBER 10

And they that know thy name will put their trust in thee: for thou, Lord, hast not forsaken them that seek thee.

—Psalm 9:10

Gracious God, help me to reflect your warmth to my family, to reflect your light that sparks their imagination and kindles their compassion. May my children know your presence through me, through the way I embody your spirit to them. Help me to change the world by creating children who exude warmth and light, dispelling the shadows around them.

OCTOBER 11

Many sorrows shall be to the wicked: but he that trusteth in the Lord, mercy shall compass him about.

—Psalm 32:10

I've got a lot of things to think about today, Lord. My mind is filled with confusion and fear, selfishness and pride. Fill it instead with that which is pure and lovely. May your truth drive out the world's lies, and I will praise you.

OCTOBER 12

The root of faith produces the flower of heart-joy. We may not at the first rejoice, but it comes in due time. We trust the Lord when we are sad, and in due season He so answers our confidence that our faith turns to fruition and we rejoice in the Lord. Doubt breeds distress, but trust means joy in the long run...

Let us meditate upon the Lord's holy name, that we may trust him the better and rejoice the more readily. He is in character holy, just, true, gracious, faithful and unchanging. Is not such a God to be trusted? He is allwise, almighty, and everywhere present; can we not cheerfully rely on him?...They that know thy name will trust thee; and they that trust thee will rejoice in thee, O Lord.

—Charles Spurgeon

OCTOBER 13

Like a river glorious is God's perfect peace,
Over all victorious in its bright increase;
Perfect, yet it floweth fuller every day,
Perfect, yet it groweth deeper all the way.
Ev'ry joy or trial falleth from above,
Traced upon our dial by the sun of love;
We may trust him fuller all for us to do
They who trust him wholly find him wholly true.
Stayed upon Jehovah, hearts are fully blest—
Finding, as he promised, perfect peace and rest.

—Frances Ridley Havergal

OCTOBER 14

The greatest burden that we have to carry in life is self. The most difficult thing we have to manage is self. . . . In laying off your burdens therefore, the first one you must get rid of is yourself. You must hand yourself and all your inward experiences, your temptations, your temperament, your . . . feelings all over into the care and keeping of our God. And leave them there. He made you, he understands you, he knows how to manage you, and you must trust him to do it.

—Hannah Whitall Smith

OCTOBER 15

I trust God's plan;
I know He made me--
What a wonder I turned out to be!
I'm not too short...
And I'm not too tall...
Just the way He planned it all.
He planned I'd be kind,
He planned I'd be good--
But I'd be even better if I could.
Sometimes I goof up;
Sometimes I get mad;
But I know I wasn't made to be bad.
I keep trying harder
To be loving and kind--
I know that's the plan God had in mind.
I like to make smiles,
I like to get hugs,
I like giving someone's heart a good tug.
It makes me feel happy
Helping out when I can--
I know for sure that was part of His plan.
In this whole wide world
There is no other me,
So I try to be the best ME I can be!

OCTOBER 16

O let him whose sorrow
no relief can find,
Trust in God, and borrow
ease for the heart and mind.
Where the mourner weeping
sheds the secret tear,
God his watch is keeping,
though none else be near.
God will never leave thee,
All thy wants he knows,
Feels the pains that grieve thee,
sees thy cares and woes.
Raise thine eyes to Heaven
when thy spirits quail,
When, by tempests driven,
heart and courage fail.
All thy woe and sadness,
in this world below,
Balance not the gladness
thou in Heaven shalt know.

—Heinrich Siegmund Oswald,
"O Let Him Whose Sorrow"

OCTOBER 17

But they that wait upon the Lord shall renew their strength; they shall mount up with wings as eagles; they shall run, and not be weary; and they shall walk, and not faint.

—Isaiah 40:31

Child, even this day, trust! And to-morrow have faith, And on all to-morrows! The darkness grow less. Trust! And each day when first gleams the dawn-breath, Awake thou to pray; God is wakeful to bless!

—Victor Hugo, "Trust in God"

OCTOBER 18

Trust in him at all times; ye people, pour out your heart before him: God is a refuge for us. Selah.

—Psalm 62:8

Living the American dream doesn't mean we don't have to act. It means we plan, we act, and then we trust in God to help us reach our goals.

OCTOBER 19

For we are saved by hope: but hope that is seen is not hope: for what a man seeth, why doth he yet hope for? But if we hope for that we see not, then do we with patience wait for it.

—Romans 8:24–25

When you see a shadow fall across our land, trust in the light of God behind it.

OCTOBER 20

For whatsoever things were written aforetime were written for our learning, that we through patience and comfort of the scriptures might have hope.

—Romans 15:4

Hope in the Lord is confident expectation that he is present, and his promises are true. If you have this hope, you also have courage and confidence that he will strengthen your heart.

OCTOBER 21

And now, Lord, what wait I for? my hope is in thee. Deliver me from all my transgressions: make me not the reproach of the foolish.

—Psalm 39:7–8

The angel of faith helps us trust God despite our circumstance.

The angel of hope helps us press on through our circumstance.

But the angel of God's love holds us in our circumstance.

OCTOBER 22

Gracious God,
I know you love me.
I know you want the best for me.
As I come before you today, you
know my aches and pains,
The things that hurt my body and the
things that pain my soul.
I ask that you heal me in whatever
way I need healing.
Open me to the power of your love.
Help me accept the healing you offer.
And let me rest gently in the palm
of your hand as a baby rests in its
mother's arms.
In your name, I pray. Amen.

OCTOBER 23

Lord,
I manage fine.
I'm healthy enough.
Yet I'm intrigued.
I'm trying to be open to the possibility
that you might be able to heal me in some
wonderful way I can't even dream of.
I'm ready to explore this further.
I don't know where it will lead, but I know
you'll be with me on this journey.
Thank you for accepting me as I am,
unbelief and all. Amen.

OCTOBER 24

I am thankful to the Lord for his gift of forgiveness. I know I am not perfect and I know I make mistakes. Grant me the wisdom and grace to know when I am wrong and to ask for forgiveness. Give me a sense of gratitude toward those who forgive my errors, and help me forgive others who have offended me.

OCTOBER 25

When you say something, Lord God, it is as good as done. It may not take place in the timing that I'd imagine or wish, but you are true to your word without fail. So when you tell me not to be anxious—but rather to pray and you will give me your peace—I'll just do that. When you say that you forgive me when I confess my sin, I'll believe that. When you tell me that I'm your child and that you rejoice over me, I'll take pleasure in that. Whatever you say, I'll not doubt it. Thank you for your great and precious promises and for your absolute trustworthiness.

OCTOBER 26

But if we hope for that we see not, then do we with patience wait for it.

—Romans 8:25

Almighty God, there are so many times when we come before you and simply confess, "We don't understand." Keep us from wasting time trying to make sense of the inscrutable! While we never want to stop mining your Word for gems of knowledge, help us find peace in the truths we can fathom and trust you with everything else.

OCTOBER 27

A lot of people these days call it karma, Lord, but I know the laws of justice and reward aren't really controlled by some vague universal force. You, the living God, declare that you are at work, giving abundantly to those who follow in your ways. You see everything we do—you see the times when we are generous to others as well as the times when we foolishly put ourselves first. You advise us to follow in your ways because it is right and good, and you promise abundant rewards. Whether our reward will come soon after a good deed or later in heaven is a mystery, but I trust you with this mystery, Lord. I know your ways are true, noble, and good, and through them, we will have all we could ever long for.

OCTOBER 28

Loving God, I confess that I worry too much. I worry about the welfare of my children. I worry about my husband's job. I worry about our budget, which buckles under the weight of our growing family. I even worry about worrying!

Forgive my doubts, my lack of faith and trust in you, O Lord. Teach me to express my family's needs to you daily in prayer and to trust in your ability to supply them.

In my heart I know you will never let us down. With you in charge of their lives, my children will want for nothing, for you take care of all your creations—even the tiniest bird and flower.

OCTOBER 29

Charity suffereth long, and is kind; charity envieth not; charity vaunteth not itself, is not puffed up.

—1 Corinthians 13:4

God,

You have given me this gift of life to care for and nurture.

May I be worthy of the task.

You have trusted me with the new responsibilities of being a parent.

May I be worthy of the task.

You have shown faith enough in me to bless me with a family.

May I be worthy of the task.

You have honored me by giving me the right to call myself "mother."

May I be worthy of the task.

Amen.

OCTOBER 30

Let us come before his presence with thanksgiving, and make a joyful noise unto him with psalms.

—Psalm 95:2

O God, stir new possibilities for our vibrant family into life among embers of trust in you. We know the Spirit fans the flame of growth so that we may become one with you, the root from which we, leaf and folk, have their source.

OCTOBER 31

Better is the end of a thing than the beginning thereof: and the patient in spirit is better than the proud in spirit. Be not hasty in thy spirit to be angry: for anger resteth in the bosom of fools.

—Ecclesiastes 7:8–9

Isn't it funny how Halloween candy can make us feel cheerful? Maybe it's the whimsy of bite-sized candy bars in their colorful foil wraps. Maybe it's the way candy corn looks, striping a pretty jar. Peanut butter cups are suddenly shaped like pumpkins; marshmallow treats take the shape of ghosts. Here's to the fanciful joys of Halloween candy!

NOVEMBER

NOVEMBER 1

Seek a quiet corner to give thanks for the saints whose day this really is. Remember those pillars of faith upon whose shoulders we stand. A marvelous opportunity—in the midst of candy and costumes—to introduce them to the children.

NOVEMBER 2

O God, we give thanks that your Son Jesus Christ, who has shared our earthly life, has now ascended to prepare our heavenly life. Grant that, through coming to know him by faith on earth, we may come to know him by sight in heaven.

—The Gelasian Sacramentary

NOVEMBER 3

Praise ye the Lord. O give thanks unto the Lord; for he is good: for his mercy endureth for ever.
Who can utter the mighty acts of the Lord? who can shew forth all his praise?

—Psalm 106:1–2

"Thanks" is the song of angels with their faces turned toward heaven.

NOVEMBER 4

In this day and age, angels are more likely to appear in street clothes than in long white robes and haloes. A neighbor who offers sound advice, a mentor who shows us how to live well, a friend who comforts us—can all be angels. If we live open to the possibility that God will use those around us to guide our way, then we may benefit from the guidance our earthly angels give. We may not hear harps playing or get goose bumps at the time, but in hindsight we may give thanks for God's angels on earth.

NOVEMBER 5

If you are feeling down and put upon, you may be in exactly the right place to receive and rejoice in the comfort of God. Nature itself breaks forth in song as it observes his mercy. So will you.

NOVEMBER 6

Every good gift and every perfect gift is from above, and cometh down from the Father of lights, with whom is no variableness, neither shadow of turning.

—James 1:17

Reasons to rejoice and give thanks are boundless.

NOVEMBER 7

Give thanks unto the Lord, call upon his name, make known his deeds among the people.

—1 Chronicles 16:8

Lifting thanks to God lifts joy in our hearts.

NOVEMBER 8

For every creature of God is good, and nothing to be refused, if it be received with thanksgiving. For it is sanctified by the word of God and prayer.

—1 Timothy 4:4–5

God calls us to celebrate; enjoy giving thanks.

NOVEMBER 9

It's hard to be pleasant these rude, road-raging days. Everyone's too immersed in their own concerns to be mannerly or kind. Encourage me to get in the first words of "please," "thanks," and "excuse me"; nudge me to be the first to take turns on the road, in the store, at work. Maybe good manners will be as catching as rude ones; may I, with your guidance, be first to pass them on.

NOVEMBER 10

Lord, you have given me the privilege to be a part of your creation. I feel blessed among women. Please make me a fit vessel for my children. Make me worthy of your trust in me, and help me to become the kind of parent you want me to be.

NOVEMBER 11

As ye have therefore received Christ Jesus the Lord, so walk ye in him: Rooted and built up in him, and stablished in the faith, as ye have been taught, abounding therein with thanksgiving.

—Colossians 2:6–7

Thanksgiving is a time for giving thanks. That's why I want to thank all of you for making my life such a blessing. To all who share our table.

NOVEMBER 12

I will praise the Lord according to his righteousness: and will sing praise to the name of the Lord most high.

—Psalm 7:17

Thank you, angels, for seeing me through. Thanks for all the caring things you do. Thanks for being aware, through times of struggle and despair, for being so faithful, so I can feel more carefree just knowing you are there.

NOVEMBER 13

Lord, you are the God who has set the foundations of the earth, who blessed Abraham with offspring "as numerous as the stars in heaven." You have blessed me, too, by giving me the treasure of my heart, my family. I pour out my thanks for these gifts, which are far above any riches the world can give. How can I praise you enough?

Heavenly Father, I never fail to come to you for help and comfort in the dark times of my life, yet I don't always remember you when my cup is overflowing. Forgive me if I seem ungrateful and take your generosity for granted. How can I forget all that you give me each day?

You bring beauty, peace, and love to my existence. My heart overflows with thanksgiving.

NOVEMBER 14

Gracious Father, I have often asked myself this question: How do I make my home a place of joy? A place where my children and husband can relax and be happy? Now I know—the answer lies with you, O Lord. Like St. Augustine, our hearts are restless until they find their home in you. Joy begins when we let you in. Life seems steadier, brighter, friendlier, safer. Your presence fills us with music. We make joyful noises when we sing your praises. All thanks to you, precious Lord, for our happy home. I will sing to you as long as I live.

NOVEMBER 15

Heavenly Father, our children receive so much, yet they seldom seem to appreciate what they have and always want more: more toys, more possessions, more food, more spending money, more attention. Their cups run over, yet expressions of thanks need to be forced from them. If they are forthcoming, they seem mechanical and insincere.

Lord, I ask for your guidance to help kindle appreciation in my children's hearts for all of their blessings. I want them to know that every good gift comes from you, that they need to thank you as well as the giver of the gift.

My children are my greatest gifts. May I always remember to express my appreciation for them at the end of each day.

NOVEMBER 16

Lord, the new command you gave your disciples, to love one another, is just what we need to challenge our children when they fight among themselves. We want to remind them that they're not showing their love when they quarrel, because love is kind, patient, and doesn't insist on its own way. Our thanks and praise to you, dear Father, for the tender messages from your word. May they take root and grow in our children's hearts.

NOVEMBER 17

Dear God,
You have blessed me with a loving, caring husband; wonderful kids; a beautiful home; friends that I can depend on; and work that I love to do. We are all healthy, and for that I give thanks. We are all happy, and for that I give thanks. We are all blessed, but no one more so than me. You have given me the gift of motherhood and of a family that means so much to me, and I will forever be grateful.

NOVEMBER 18

Give thanks to God, for he is good. Even when we are struggling, God is there to help us. Even when we are feeling lost and alone, God stands beside us and shows us we are loved. Even when we are sure we cannot go on, God picks us up and carries us. Give thanks to God.

NOVEMBER 19

And it came to pass, when he had made an end of speaking unto Saul, that the soul of Jonathan was knit with the soul of David, and Jonathan loved him as his own soul.

—1 Samuel 18:1

Dear God, David was an enemy of Saul—and yet Saul's own son Jonathan became David's close friend. Please help me to remember that you can unite even unlikely people in friendship.

NOVEMBER 20

After a routine dental procedure went awry, Megan became very ill. She contracted blood poisoning and the pain in her jaw was beyond anything she'd ever experienced. Thanks to antibiotics and sound medical care, Megan recovered, but now, even months later, when she wakes pain-free she still gives thanks to God. "It took an extreme situation to remind me of the importance of thanking God; being grateful inspires joy, and I feel closer to God than ever," Megan says. Dear Lord, I understand how important it is to give thanks to you. It draws me closer to you, and is good for my heart.

NOVEMBER 21

Now thanks be unto God, which always causeth us to triumph in Christ, and maketh manifest the savour of his knowledge by us in every place.

—2 Corinthians 2:14

Battle metaphors are common in scripture, with believers cast as soldiers in a never-ending war against the enemies of God. The Apostle Peter says, “be vigilant; because your adversary the devil, as a roaring lion, walketh about” (1 Peter 5:8). By God’s strength, however, we “overcometh the world” (1 John 5:4).

What a strange weapon, then, this “savour of his knowledge in every place.” Some translations phrase it as “fragrance.” We do not trust in horses and chariots (Psalm 20:7), but in the name and power of God. We “wrestle not against flesh and blood,” but advance with the “gospel of peace” and the “sword of the Spirit” (Ephesians 6:10–18). And so the sweet savour, or fragrance, of him is diffused in all the world.

NOVEMBER 22

The grace I need today, God, is the grace to believe that you are altogether sufficient. My thoughts and my strength are not enough to meet the temptations that I face. But you are able, and you are near. And that is enough.

NOVEMBER 23

I pray all the time when I am suffering or facing some obstacle in life. I get on my knees and ask for God's help whenever things are not going well. For me, the challenge is to remember to pray to God in thanksgiving when everything is going well. Does God only want me to come talk with him when I have a complaint or a problem? God, I promise to come to you to celebrate blessings as well as lessons. I promise to show my gratitude as easily as I show my fears. Thank you, God, for being there no matter which way I come to you.

NOVEMBER 24

And he shall stand and feed in the strength of the Lord.

—Micah 5:4

Christ is prophesied as the great "ruler in Israel" (verse 2). As King, however, he does not merely sit and rule. He stands and feeds his flock. This suggests all that a shepherd can do—guarding, tending, nurturing, and feeding, active and purposeful in the care of his church.

C H. Spurgeon puts it this way: "His eyes never slumber, and his hands never rest; his heart never ceases to beat with love, and his shoulders are never weary of carrying his people's burdens." What a model for leaders and what a comfort for followers! For this reason, "we thy people and sheep of thy pasture will give thee thanks for ever: we will shew forth thy praise to all generations" (Psalm 79:13).

NOVEMBER 25

Lord, we lift up our marriage to you with thanks for the gift you gave us when you first brought us together: it isn't as fresh and new as it was when you created it for us, Lord, so we ask your blessing again. Wrap the life we share in your protective arms so that the world will never be able to tear us apart. Fill us anew with the precious love you gave us for one another. Hold us firmly in your eternal love. Amen.

NOVEMBER 26

Let us, on the day set aside for this purpose, give thanks to the ruler of the universe for the strength which He has vouchsafed us to carry on our daily labors and for the hope that lives within us of the coming of a day when peace and the productive activities of peace shall reign on every continent.

—President Franklin D. Roosevelt

NOVEMBER 27

Be it health or be it leisure,
Be it skill we have to give,
Still in spending it for others
Christians only really live.
Not in having or receiving,
But in giving, there is bliss;
He who has no other pleasure
Ever may rejoice in this.

—Author Unknown

NOVEMBER 28

Praise ye the Lord: for it is good to sing praises unto our God; for it is pleasant; and praise is comely.

—Psalm 147:1

Our strengths were given to us to help us serve. God rejoices when we change our "How can I help myself?" attitude to one of "How can I help others?"

NOVEMBER 29

We trust the Lord when we are sad, and in due season he so answers our confidence that our faith turns to fruition and we rejoice in the Lord. Doubt breeds distress, but trust means joy.

—Charles Spurgeon

NOVEMBER 30

I will praise the name of God with a song, and will magnify him with thanksgiving.

—Psalm 69:30

Angels rejoice, worship, and love. They probably whoop and holler, as well. We can only imagine, for now, the excitement in their hometown.

DECEMBER

DECEMBER 1

Blessed Father, when we think of joy, we often think of things that are new—a new day, a new baby, a new love, a new beginning, the promise of a new home with God in heaven. Rejoicing in these things originates with having joy in you who make all things new. Rather than relying on earthly pleasures to provide happiness, the Scriptures command that we rejoice in you and in each new day you bring. Joy is a celebration of the heart that goes beyond circumstances to the very foundation of joy—the knowledge that we are loved by you. Help us rejoice in your teachings. Amen.

DECEMBER 2

Shopping, wrapping, traveling, cooking. So much to do this season as we hurry toward the manger, answering God's call as did those folk so long ago, to go, believe, and do. Practice the notes of the carol, for soon it will be time to sing out "Gloria!" at what we'll see and hear.

DECEMBER 3

Therefore the Lord himself shall give you a sign; Behold, a virgin shall conceive, and bear a son, and shall call his name Immanuel.

—Isaiah 7:14

Our spirits rejoice when the Lord speaks to us.

DECEMBER 4

For God so loved the world, that he gave his only begotten Son, that whosoever believeth in him should not perish, but have everlasting life.

—John 3:16

Rejoice in the glory of God.

DECEMBER 5

But when the fulness of the time was come, God sent forth his Son, made of a woman, made under the law,

To redeem them that were under the law, that we might receive the adoption of sons.

—Galatians 4:4–5

Joy unites the hearts of all who rejoice in Jesus.

DECEMBER 6

And the Word was made flesh, and dwelt among us, (and we beheld his glory, the glory as of the only begotten of the Father,) full of grace and truth.

—John 1:14

All who look to God will rejoice in the blessing of his salvation.

DECEMBER 7

Lord, do you have a victory song you sing over me when your ways triumph in my life? Do you exult when your truth and love prevail in me and you put down those age-old enemies of bitterness, hatred, resentment, and the like? I sometimes forget that you are not just calm and stoic. You rejoice over my victories and you grieve when I wander away from you. You welcome me with gladness as I come to you today, and you renew me in your love. You are truly wonderful to me, Lord.

DECEMBER 8

Zacharias was promised a son. He and his wife Elizabeth would be the parents of a great prophet, John the Baptist. "Thou shalt have joy and gladness," (Luke 1:14) the angel told him, but Zacharias could not believe this. And the angel took away his voice until the baby was born (verses 13–18).

The 19th-century preacher Charles Spurgeon says we must treat the promises of God as "a check payable to order. It is given to the believer with the view of bestowing upon him some good thing." Those who do not cash the check prove nothing about the value of the check, he points out. Like Zacharias, we can fail to treat the promises of God like money in the bank.

DECEMBER 9

For the wages of sin is death; but the gift of God is eternal life through Jesus Christ our Lord.

—Romans 6:23

DECEMBER 10

For unto us a child is born, unto us a son is given: and the government shall be upon his shoulder: and his name shall be called Wonderful, Counsellor, The mighty God, The everlasting Father, The Prince of Peace.

—Isaiah 9:6

Even before opening your eyes, listen to that inner voice inviting you to yet another glorious adventure at the hands of a child. God is holding both of you.

DECEMBER 11

Gracious is the Lord, and righteous; yea, our God is merciful.

—Psalm 116:5

DECEMBER 12

Encourage your child to learn, to master, to question—to try. It may feel like a big adventure and maybe even a huge risk, but you can relax, knowing that God is blessing the undertaking and providing the fuel for the journey.

DECEMBER 13

Behold, I will send my messenger, and he shall prepare the way before me: and the Lord, whom ye seek, shall suddenly come to his temple, even the messenger of the covenant, whom ye delight in: behold, he shall come, saith the Lord of hosts.

—Malachi 3:1

Seeking God is an adventure with the happiest of endings.

DECEMBER 14

John to the seven churches which are in Asia: Grace be unto you, and peace, from him which is, and which was, and which is to come; and from the seven Spirits which are before his throne.

—Revelation 1:4

DECEMBER 15

Connected in memory to holidays past, like links in a colorful paper chain decorating the tree, we celebrate another advent. Some recollections are happy and pleasant, others sad and empty, yet each brings us to this new starting point, as fresh and full of promise as an egg about to hatch. Make all things new this holiday, even old memories, for this is the season of second chances.

DECEMBER 16

Explorer God,

You have put within us a spirit of adventure to move us beyond the immediate and to explore even our most familiar environment to its fullest potential. May each day become an adventure of people, tasks, places, and responsibilities. And when I feel gray and lifeless, may your Spirit remind me that each day brings its own gifts and that the best is yet to be.

DECEMBER 17

Heavenly Father, the writer of Proverbs values knowledge and education, and so do I. Please enable me to impart my love of learning to my children so they can meet the challenges of the schoolroom with confidence and a sense of adventure.

Give me the insight to know when to help them with schoolwork and when to back off. Show me how to strike a balance between pressing for higher achievement and accepting what is accomplished. Above all, make me an encourager not a hindrance to the learning process.

Lord, you are the great teacher. Teach me to inspire my children to reach their highest potentials and use their education to glorify you.

DECEMBER 18

Through the tender mercy of
our God; whereby the dayspring
from on high hath visited us.

—Luke 1:78

DECEMBER 19

In the lights and glimmer of modern Christmas decorations we see a tiny speck of brilliance that is the reality angels see, share, and return to when their task on earth is complete. It's a brilliance we can one day see for ourselves when our task is done as well.

DECEMBER 20

I heard the bells on Christmas day

Their old familiar carols play,

And wild and sweet the words repeat

Of peace on earth, good will to men.

Then pealed the bells more loud and deep:

God is not dead, nor doth he sleep;

The wrong shall fail, the right prevail,

With peace on earth, good will to men.

—Henry Wadsworth Longfellow

DECEMBER 21

There's more, much more to Christmas
Than candlelight and cheer;
It's the spirit of sweet friendship
That brightens all the year;
It's thoughtfulness and kindness,
It's hope reborn again,
For peace, for understanding
And for good will to men!

DECEMBER 22

So remember while December
Brings the only Christmas Day,
In the year let there be Christmas
In the things you do and say.
Wouldn't life be worth the living,
Wouldn't dreams be coming true,
If we kept the Christmas spirit
All the whole year through?

—Author Unknown

DECEMBER 23

For unto you is born this day
in the city of David a Saviour,
which is Christ the Lord.

—Luke 2:11

May you have peace this Christmas and be guided by the strength of the Lord in the coming year.

DECEMBER 24

And she shall bring forth a son, and thou shalt call his name Jesus: for he shall save his people from their sins.

—Matthew 1:21

Christmas is God's gift to us. May its blessings bring you joy and peace the whole year through.

DECEMBER 25

God, on this most blessed day, I cannot contain the love in my heart for all you have given me: my spouse, my child, my family, and my friends. My heart is bursting with joy. Today I will celebrate the birth of your son and the birth of newfound happiness in my soul. Today I will honor the love you gave to the world and the love I, in turn, give to my own. Today I will rejoice in the gifts you have bestowed upon the earth and the gifts you have given to me. Thank you, God, for your love, for your light, for your son, for this day of glorious good tidings. Amen.

DECEMBER 26

Disaster can strike at any time without warning to anyone anywhere. Our lives can change dramatically in one unexpected moment, but in the worst times of our lives, we can lean on family, friends, and even strangers who reach out to us. Yet, even more importantly, we can turn to God, who is always there for us during our darkest hours. He will never fail us, never let us down, and never turn away from us when we cry out to him.

DECEMBER 27

After the storm, they cautiously push open their closet door and creep from their hiding place. How bad is it? They see destruction everywhere. Nothing left untouched, except for one safe spot—the closet in which the whole family crouched, pressed tight together, frightened, holding one another, praying. One thing remains, upright and safe—their hiding place in time of trouble, their sanctuary, the right place to be.

DECEMBER 28

No darkness is black enough to hide you, Lord, for there is always light even if I sometimes misplace it. Just when I'm ready to give up, there it shines through caregivers, family, friends; through my renewed energy to choose treatments and recovery. I'm absolutely certain you are the sender of this light.

DECEMBER 29

Though thy beginning was small, yet thy latter end should greatly increase.

—Job 8:7

Bless this family, Lord.
This is my fervent prayer.
Hold us safely in your arms
And sustain us by your care.

DECEMBER 30

The slate is clean, Lord, the calendar as bare as the Christmas tree. Bless the New Year that beckons. We sing of you as help in ages past but need to know you as hope for years to come. Help us face what we must, celebrate every triumph we can, and make any changes we need. We're celebrating to the fullest this whistle-blowing, toast-raising moment, for it is the threshold between the old and new in us.

DECEMBER 31

Lord, please bless this new year! I'm already seeing my calendar fill up with obligations and social events, but I want to take time this day—and every day—to focus on you. I ask you to bless my endeavors this year, to guide me to the people you want me to have in my life and activities you have in mind for me. Let me never be so busy and frazzled that I don't see the signs of your grace around me.